UnHealthcare

A Manifesto for Health Assurance

HEMANT TANEJA & STEPHEN KLASKO

WITH KEVIN MANEY

Copyright © 2020 Commure, Inc.

All rights reserved. No part of this book may be reproduced or used in any manner without written permission of the copyright owner except for the use of quotations in a book review.

First Edition: June 2020

Design by Michelle Gruyé-Hallam

Print ISBN: 978-1-71699-651-1
eBook ISBN: 978-1-71693-606-7

Published by Hemant Taneja and Stephen Klasko

www.healthassurance.ai
contact@healthassurance.ai

FROM HEMANT TANEJA

To my dad, Shiv Kumar Taneja

FROM STEVE KLASKO

To Lynne, David, Jill, Evan and Juliet..., may you thrive without health problems getting in the way...and to my wife Colleen, thank you for tolerating my frequent trips to the other coast

TABLE OF CONTENTS

Foreword: Care in a Post-Covid World — vii

1. A Silicon Valley Entrepreneur and an East Coast Healthcare CEO — 1
2. Consumer-Centric Health Assurance — 11
3. How Healthcare Can Reinvent Itself...If It's Not Already Too Late — 29
4. The Case Against Health Insurance as We Know It — 43
5. Policy for Health Assurance — 58
6. Company Design for Health Assurance — 78
7. Health Assurance and the Next Pandemic — 94

Acknowledgments — 105

Index — 109

FOREWORD

Care in a Post-Covid World

We had just finished this book—well, a more innocent version of this book—when the Covid-19 crisis started steamrolling around the globe. We hit pause, knowing that Covid-19 would radically change the healthcare landscape.

Within a month, we could see that everything we originally wrote about was accelerating because of Covid. We were writing about a new category of care that we thought would evolve over five or ten years. Instead, the future is rushing to us. One simple example is virtual doctor visits, often called telehealth. A few months ago, it seemed that consumers and healthcare professionals would slowly come around to the idea. Covid made it necessary immediately. Now we see that virtual visits are effective for patients and can make the healthcare system more resilient and responsive. There's no going back. The concept of "seeing a doctor" has changed for good.

On the flip side, it's become painfully obvious that if a new kind of care we call *health assurance*—explained in detail in this book—had been in place before Covid, the crisis might have had a different trajectory. An important driver of health assurance is data—every person's ability to get continuous, real-time data about their health so they can keep themselves healthy and out of doctor's offices and hospitals. That data, once in the cloud, can also be anonymized and analyzed for population health.

If tens of millions of people all over the world had been using health assurance services by January 2020, the data could've helped officials spot the outbreak early or see clusters developing, and take actions to minimize the impact. It could have saved the lives of heroic first responders, doctors and nurses, who would have fewer cases to treat and more advanced information about patients coming to them.

At the same time, individuals using health assurance services could've been confident that their health was being constantly monitored by software. The service could've looked for patterns in a user's data that indicated the user had caught the virus, then provided instructions about what to do about it.

One story that surfaced in April 2020 gives a glimpse of how health assurance technologies can help track a pandemic. A company called Kinsa sells an internet-connected smart thermometer for consumers. It comes with an app, so you can track your temperature and get information about how to treat the fever. But the underlying purpose is to gather data from all the Kinsa thermometers to see global patterns of fevers. As the Covid outbreak gained steam, Kinsa had about two million users—not an enormous number, relatively. Yet it was able to predict hotspots or see where public health measures were being effective, often ahead of the U.S. Centers for Disease Control and Prevention. "If you want to know where disease is spreading, you have to know the symptoms," Kinsa founder Inder Singh told CNBC. "The best way was to piggyback off a tool [people] already had."

If data patterns from two million thermometer users can get ahead of government agencies, imagine the value of data from tens of millions of consumers using devices that track everything from heart rate to mental health, blood sugar levels and sleep patterns. We're not saying that health assurance would prevent the next pandemic. But it would give healthcare professionals and governments better tools for containing dangerous new viruses and keeping people healthy if outbreaks occur.

Over the next couple of years, health assurance technologies will become enormously helpful as governments try to restart economies. At this writing, experts are saying we'll see a prolonged period of loosening and tightening of restrictions on movement and gathering. Restrictions will loosen; we'll resume a modicum of normal life; the virus will resurface; and restrictions will tighten again until the virus is contained. To pull that off well, governments will need rich, real-time data about citizens' health. The more health assurance technologies permeate the market, the more health data we'll have, and that will allow officials to make decisions on restrictions quickly and accurately. We are absolutely confident that health assurance can be a game-changer during this period, and may help us all get back sooner to some version of normal.

We had other reasons to hit pause, too.

Steve was right at the epicenter of the Covid crisis, running fourteen hospitals in Philadelphia and New Jersey. He spent lots of time thinking about what would have been if the principles in this book had been enacted. While not enough can be said about the front-line healthcare heroes at Jefferson and throughout the country, data was scarce and not analyzed in a coordinated fashion. Each state, sometimes counties within a state, had its own strategies. Jefferson Health went from 50 telehealth visits a day to 3,000, but many health systems did not have the bandwidth to offer telehealth.

In cities such as Philadelphia, Covid highlighted the fact that a large percentage of the population does not have broadband or computers at home or smartphones in their pockets. Those people could not use telehealth if they wanted to. If the new era of health assurance is to be built on connectivity to consumers, we need policies that ensure everyone has the necessary access. Covid-19 hit those who can afford it least.

Hemant is the co-founder of two health assurance technology companies, Commure and Livongo, and an investor in numerous other technology companies. As the economy shut down, Hemant first worked with his companies to help them stabilize, endure, and keep their employees safe. Since many of his portfolio companies serve small business, Hemant also dove into helping small-business clients and customers remain successful.

He already had come to believe that healthcare is the single most important area where entrepreneurs can make a difference this decade. Covid took that thinking to the next level. He realized that this is a moment like the introduction of Apple's iPhone, when a new universe of possibilities opens up. It's a fast-forward into a future where technology can fix the lack of resilience in healthcare—a problem that hadn't been apparent before Covid.

The pandemic also strengthened Steve and Hemant's view that real change will come as tech entrepreneurs and the traditional healthcare ecosystem work together instead of against each other—a theme you will see repeated throughout this manifesto.

What we've all learned is that dangerous viruses like Covid-19 will happen again, and our only choice is to innovate our way to a society that can get ahead of outbreaks and manage them. Otherwise, we will continue to lose lives and devastate the global economy every time one of these viruses emerges.

This book is our attempt to spark that innovation and inspire health professionals, entrepreneurs, policymakers and other leaders to take action.

Hemant Taneja
Stephen Klasko
Kevin Maney
April 2020

1

A Silicon Valley Entrepreneur and an East Coast Healthcare CEO

In the best of all worlds, healthcare would not exist.

If our bodies and minds stayed healthy until the day we suddenly expired, we would happily do without doctors, pills, hospitals and insurance companies. That has never rung true more than now, in the wake of Covid-19.

The next best thing would be to have a system designed to help us need as little healthcare as possible—to help us mostly forget about doctors, pills, hospitals and insurance companies. True "healthcare," even for the chronically ill, would disappear into our everyday lives, helping us stay as well as possible without having to think too much about our health.

Such a system would make basic health more easily available to all, at less cost, and relieve doctors and hospitals from mundane burdens so they could focus on critical problems and saving lives. The system could even help officials identify dangerous viruses early, so they could keep them from turning into crises.

Such a system would be new and different. It would be *health assurance.*

Health assurance is new. It's a category of consumer-centric, data-driven, cloud-based healthcare designed to help us stay well, so we need as little "sick care" as possible. It's built on principles of open technology standards, empathetic user design and responsible AI. It is a radically new kind of experience that works as easily as most of our other consumer experiences. It promises to shift healthcare from its current irrational economics to more rational, free-market economics. That shift can drive costs down while improving outcomes—better health, more empathy, fewer mistakes, less frustration.

Everyone wants to "fix" healthcare—even people who work in healthcare. There had been wide agreement that the U.S. healthcare system was not working for most people, and the Covid-19 pandemic laid bare its troubles. The best way forward now is to encourage new companies and inventions to bloom in the health assurance space. That is far better than passing legislation that would only find another way to pay for the old, expensive, frustrating healthcare industry.

Healthcare must be as easy to access as Google Maps. The pre-Covid system was built around the concept of scarcity—that there were not enough physicians, hospital beds, medical devices or drugs to go around, so these things had to be expensive and hard to get. By contrast, many other industries have by now transformed from scarcity to abundance:[1] Instead of trudging to a store to pay money for a physical map that can only be printed in limited quantities, every person on earth can tap a phone screen and get a map instantly for free… and that map even has GPS that routes you around traffic jams. It's time for healthcare to transform from scarcity to abundance through technology.

---

[1] As described by Peter Diamandis and Steven Kotler in their book *Abundance: The Future is Better Than You Think*, Free Press, 2012.

It's ridiculous that you've had to use a telephone to get a doctor's appointment two weeks out even though you could buy a car in ten minutes through an app and have it delivered to your driveway. We've reinvented commerce, community and content online. Now it's time to reinvent care.

We need builders and innovators to partner with healthcare professionals to transform the industry so it stops making us conform to an old healthcare model—and instead makes care conform to us. It's the difference between retailers of the last century making you drive to their stores to look for a product they may not carry, walk their aisles and stand in line at a cash register versus Amazon getting to know you and giving you a personalized store anywhere, on any device, at any time.

Technology developed over the past dozen years—mobile phones, the cloud, artificial intelligence and much more—creates forces no industry can evade, and that includes healthcare. To see the early outlines of a new model, look to startups such as Livongo (an AI-driven model for chronic care), Commure (a platform for medical applications) and some familiar direct-to-consumer companies like Warby Parker (prescription glasses bought online) and Ro (online care and drugs). The biggest players in technology—Apple, Amazon, Google, Microsoft—are investing heavily in this space, and so many more startups and innovations are coming.

This new model will be so different from the old one that we shouldn't even call it healthcare. That label is tied to the past, and a misnomer. Anyone in the healthcare industry will tell you that they're really in a "sick care" industry designed primarily to help people only after they've developed problems.

The term *health assurance* captures the spirit of this new sector that provides easy access to services and technology aimed at ensuring we stay well.

Every politician, doctor, healthcare industry executive, employer, entrepreneur and consumer should embrace health assurance, which promises to be more profitable, more efficient, more sustainable and more cost-effective than today's healthcare—and infinitely better for consumers. Crucially, health assurance will give the world data and knowledge so that we have a better chance of defeating or containing future contagions.

The health assurance space will give birth to more than ten to fifteen $100-billion companies. The $3 trillion in annual health spending in the U.S. will shrink and be captured by these new companies. The most successful of them will come from creative partnerships between technology companies and professionals in traditional healthcare. The quicker the two worlds merge, the sooner we will stop wasting time on overly-complicated ways to give people access to a fragmented, expensive and inequitable healthcare system.

It's not productive to blame the vast majority of people in healthcare. In fact, many of them are heroes. They risked their lives—and some lost their lives—saving millions of us from a frightening pandemic. They were instead often frustrated by a system that was fundamentally broken. Most of them want to be part of the solution.

The current healthcare system is a mass-production model that was right for its time. It scaled up and delivered healthcare to an exploding population, reflecting a fundamental belief in much of the world that even the poorest people should have access to care. That scaled-up model improved the average lifespan in the U.S. from 70 years of age in 1960 to nearly 80 today. But our model is past its prime and becoming its own worst enemy, and the consequences of not transforming to a new paradigm are dire.

Most debates about healthcare among U.S. politicians center around the best ways to have American citizens afford the old healthcare system. But asking who pays—the government, consumers or employers—is asking the wrong question. The right question is: How do we enable risk-takers in technology and healthcare to partner and create a transformative approach to lifelong health for all?

Of course, there are enormous obstacles to overcome. But our healthcare system is already in a downward spiral of shrinking margins and exploding costs. Trying to fix it would be like putting a coat of paint on a crumbling building.

Getting from here to there is what this call to action is about, and why we found ourselves working together to start new-era health assurance companies.

* * *

For years tech entrepreneurs from all over the world have started hundreds of companies to try to disrupt traditional healthcare. Some have made well-designed apps or clever devices, and some are becoming quite successful. Other companies only added to the burden on physicians, pushing them to spend time on a computer screen instead of with patients. Yet these new companies barely changed America's monolithic healthcare system. The apps and devices—even those getting serious traction—got stuck on the fringes, still far from most people's core healthcare experience.

Why? Because the two sectors—technology and medicine—have not effectively worked together.

In Silicon Valley, too many startups launched by engineers bring in some healthcare advisors but never really understand the complexity of the system. The startups tend to attack just one aspect of a giant, interlocking industry that goes into self-protection mode when outsiders invade. The usual Silicon Valley mentality of "move fast, break things, get a ton of users, then figure out the business model" doesn't work in healthcare for myriad reasons, which we'll get into later.

So, when it comes to reinventing healthcare, the technorati have mostly failed.

Meanwhile, the healthcare community is well-aware of its problems. Before Covid, it tried for years to create technology that could change the healthcare experience.

But whether healthcare people start a company or build technology inside an existing institution, they often hire some engineers and direct them to try to improve the efficiency of something the industry already does. That might save some money and boost margins, but it will never drive real change that will bend the cost and quality curve. It will never fix what's really broken.

During the Covid pandemic, we saw how far behind healthcare is. Most providers were not ready to increase their use of telehealth, and relatively few physicians and nurses had been trained in virtual visits. Electronic medical records were fragmented and there was no natural repository for aggregated data or mutually agreed-upon population health analytics. If healthcare in 2020 had been as digitized as the financial industry, everyone would've had a lot more information to help in fighting Covid.

The not-so-secret dirty secret of the old healthcare system is that almost everybody makes more money when more people are sick. (Well, until something like Covid overwhelms the system. Covid nearly broke the system and led to disarray and financial loss in the sector.) It's hard to get big institutions excited about changing something when their revenue depends upon not changing it. So the healthcare industry failed to transform itself.

Consumers of healthcare also bear some responsibility for the lack of change. We became addicted to the drug of "other people's money"—usually in the form of an employer's health insurance or Medicare or some other program—paying for our healthcare. And we kept forgiving a broken model because it was all we knew. In this era of social media and digital everything, we've made almost every other industry serve consumers better, but haven't demanded that of healthcare, thinking it's different. It's not. We all must demand that this industry treat us like intelligent consumers.

The two of us—Hemant Taneja and Steve Klasko—came together in the spirit of partnership we think is critical to building a health assurance system. We want to be one of those teams that blends technology and healthcare and drives change.

Hemant brings to this a long history of investing in and founding tech companies aimed at transforming hard-to-transform industries, like energy and banking. His operating thesis is that the global economy is going through a profound transformation driven by technologies developed over the past decade: mobile platforms, social media, cloud computing, artificial intelligence, robotics. These technologies make it possible to efficiently and profitably offer highly personalized products and services at scale—which means every individual can feel like the product or service revolves around him or her. Such a product beats a generic mass-market offering every time.

Every industry is feeling this profound change. That's why Airbnb (a place to stay that feels just right for you) is beating the market for hotels (the same room for everybody). It's why Khan Academy (online courses just right for each student) is often proving to be a better way to learn than sitting in a classroom lecture (the same material for all the students). In sector after sector, the clunky, physical, costly, mass-market, mass-production business model is yielding to a digital, mass-personalized, nimble, low-cost, business model called "unscaling."

The unscale model asks: What can I build that makes each individual happy in an individual way? That's a big change from last century's corporate mindset: What can I build that I can sell to the greatest number of people in the same way?

Hemant brought that thinking to healthcare by founding Commure, a technology platform built to unscale healthcare.

Healthcare insiders need to be on board with unscaling, and Steve is determined to show how. In fact, he has experienced both the thesis and the antithesis of unscaling—a balancing act we like to call Klasko's Conundrum.

Jefferson, the institution Steve runs, had no external growth for almost thirty years. In the 2010s it became one of the fastest-growing academic medical centers in the nation: six mergers and acquisitions in five years took it from three hospitals to fourteen, with four more in the works. That sounds like scaling up, not unscaling, but Jefferson had to scale up because the healthcare industry's shaky economics meant that the only path to survival was merging operations to cut costs and become an essential asset for the community. Steve must manage the difficult task of scaling up Jefferson to survive now, so Jefferson can be in a position to unscale later.

Jefferson's mission under Steve has been "healthcare with no address." He wants, "every person in the greater Philadelphia area to be able to access healthcare the same seamless, easy way that they access and experience every other consumer good." In other words, Jefferson's success will mean that five years from now, if someone comes to Philadelphia and asks, "Where's Jefferson?" no one will be able to point to a building. Rather, Jefferson will be defined by the care it gives. That's unscaling at its best.

We believe all big healthcare institutions must manage the balance between scaling up now and unscaling later. The industry will be wrestling with Klasko's Conundrum for years.

How did we realize the power of bringing our two communities together? It started because of a company Hemant helped launch in 2014, Livongo. The co-founder was Glen Tullman, who ran Allscripts, which makes software for writing prescriptions electronically. Steve knew Glen personally and, because his hospitals were Allscripts customers, professionally. When Livongo launched as a new way to care for people who have diabetes, Steve agreed to have Jefferson try it. He was skeptical at first, but found that Jefferson's patients loved Livongo's service, and that it helped them manage their conditions. Patients were happier, Steve's costs were less for that population, and "healthcare with no address" went from philosophy to reality.

Livongo is an early health assurance company that went public in 2019 at a valuation of about $2.5 billion. The success of Livongo at Jefferson turned on a light bulb for both of us: Hemant realized that tech companies need to understand and integrate with health systems in order to truly change things, and Steve understood that if he can help a new wave of health tech companies take root, his industry has a chance of transforming before it crumbles under the weight of its own bad economics.

Since Livongo, our two camps have partnered in more ways. Steve has been advising some of the health tech companies, such as Color Genomics, that Hemant previously funded. Now we're both invested in and helping to build an ambitious health-assurance tech platform, Commure. We've also worked on an online, AI-driven mental health company called Mindstrong.

But this book isn't about us or our companies—it's about creating conditions so a thousand Livongos and Commures and Mindstrongs can bloom. We want to show how to get from what we've got now to where we need to be. It's important for everyone as individuals and, as Covid showed, critical for society as a whole.

The industry's transition will open up enormous opportunities for technology and healthcare practitioners, entrepreneurs, executives and companies. The healthcare debate often sounds like we have to choose between distasteful options. That's wrong. There's another path that doesn't rely on disruption or austerity; it is about creating something new and exciting—like moving from the days of train travel to the era of jet airliners.

2

Consumer-Centric Health Assurance

The U.S. healthcare system has been a mess for decades. Many entrepreneurs have tried to shift the industry toward a more effective, less costly consumer experience, but they have failed. So it's easy to understand the pervasive mentality: Why even try? Entrenched forces will always win.

That's not true anymore. Much has changed in the past couple of years, teeing up what Intel's late, great CEO Andy Grove would call a strategic inflection point.[2]

A handful of health and medical startups developed enough traction to make an impact and go public. Many of those companies have been creating business models that others can learn from or improve on. AI has become powerful enough to play a significant role in everyone's health. Standards such as FHIR—which stands for Fast Healthcare Interoperability Resources (pronounced "fire")—have emerged since 2018 to allow health apps to share data and, in March

---

[2] Andy Grove described this in his book *Only the Paranoid Survive: How to Exploit the Crisis Points That Challenge Every Company*, Currency, 1999.

2020, the U.S. Department of Health and Human Services (HHS) introduced new rules aimed at giving patients more secure access to and control over their health data. Consumer attitudes have been shifting: Because of the expense and limitations of traditional health insurance, more consumers are paying for more of their care out of pocket, driving them to demand better experiences. Policymakers are proposing radical change. It's even fair to say that the healthcare industry is sick of itself.

As all of that pressure on the old model built up, Covid became the tipping point. The complexities of insurance and billing became a joke amid the scramble to save lives. The dangers to all when only some have adequate care became vivid—the poorest person with a virus can infect the richest. Ancient resistance to trying new things in medicine vanished. The desire to do anything to stay out of a hospital or doctor's office gripped us all.

In short, Covid accelerated a desire for change. Now is the time to make that happen. This is, essentially, the iPhone moment for healthcare—a flash in time that opens up a universe of new possibilities. All of the conditions were present; now Covid is making it happen.

If you are a product-centric entrepreneur, suspend disbelief and think about reinventing healthcare the way the tech industry thinks about reinventing nearly every other industry. Believe that if you create a great user experience of value, you have an open road toward building a multibillion-dollar success like Airbnb or Slack.

So, then...what could you build?

You'd want to build something that helps people use as little "sick care"—i.e., traditional healthcare—as possible. Again: Nobody wants to go to a doctor or think about their illness. People want an affordable, easy, intuitive, unobtrusive way to stay healthy and manage any health problems as conveniently as possible.

In other words, you wouldn't build a healthcare company. You would, instead, build a health assurance company. You'd want consumers to understand that you are not buffing the edges of a failing old experience, but creating an entirely new experience.

That new experience must built on data. Not data the way the old healthcare industry thinks about it. But rather data from what we might call a real-time, always-on, perpetual digital physical.

The annual physical used to be the foundation of a doctor–patient relationship. Consider how flawed that is in this era, when we check jet engines, cars and factories with measurement systems that can spot a breakdown before it becomes serious—but can't tell if someone has a life-threatening virus until symptoms appear.

The typical physical is primarily a data collection opportunity. Your physician takes your blood pressure, weighs you, takes your temperature, does an EKG, draws blood for lab tests, looks in some orifices and pokes a few others, and then has about five minutes to ask how you're doing. The data comes with no context—no sense, for instance, of what your heart rate or breathing pattern is every day and whether it's showing troubling patterns. The data connects to no other data about your life—nothing about what you eat, where you've been, who you've met, how much stress you've been under. So, basically, the physician knows the state of your health only during the short time you're in the examination room. And the physician has little time to talk to you, because he or she has to stay on schedule.

An entirely new kind of "physical"—rich in data and deeply rooted in human empathy—will become the new starting place for your health assurance.

Some of the most essential data is in your DNA. We're in the midst of a genomics revolution. The cost of sending in a bit of saliva for pulling out data from your DNA has gone so far, so fast, that consumers now do it for sites like Ancestry.com just to find out where they came from. One of our companies, Color, began doing inexpensive genetic tests for individuals or, in some cases, all employees at a company, as a basis for creating a data-rich record of each person's make-up. 23andMe, a consumer-oriented pioneer in this space, now has more than 10 million users, and its kits are sold in CVS and Walgreens. Clearly, a new industry is forming.

Within a few years, genetic tests will be as routine as a blood test used to check cholesterol, except people will analyze their DNA only once because the results never change. It won't be long before everyone has their DNA tested at birth, making it part of each person's health record for life.

Your genome tells doctors whether you have a predisposition for certain cancers or other diseases, and gives all sorts of clues about how to care for you, including what drugs are likely to be effective for you. It can even guide you to understand how fast you metabolize caffeine—important to know if, say, you have insomnia. And it might provide clues about how to help each individual fight off a new virus.

Other basic layers of data will include your microbiome and deep blood tests. Your microbiome is the bacteria in your gut, which is unique to every individual. Companies are emerging to analyze the microbiome and make it an important piece of your medical data. Another batch of companies are taking the blood test to new places, pulling data never before accessible. Grail has raised $1.6 billion and is on course to offer a blood test that can detect cancer with few false positives and identify the location of the tumor.

While genomics, biome and blood yield static data, connected devices will record and analyze a constant flow of data in real time. *Which* devices and *what* data will depend on the person. Some people will never want to wear a gadget that records any physiological data.

Others will want everything measured, maybe wearing a connected watch loaded with apps that constantly record steps taken, heart rate, hours of sleep, body temperature and so on. A startup, Spire, makes a tiny tag that is sewn into the band of your underwear and tracks your breathing patterns—it can help detect asthma, panic attacks, even drug overdoses that slow breathing. Of course, breathing was an issue during the Covid pandemic, and something like Spire could have played a significant role if more people had had access to the tags.

Some app may even keep an eye on the groceries you order online or meals that come from your delivery services in order to get a snapshot of your eating patterns. People with chronic conditions such as diabetes or hypertension might use a specialized device that tracks blood sugar or blood pressure. Our company, Livongo, is doing this for people with diabetes and is expanding the model to help people with other chronic conditions. The possibilities for businesses here are almost endless.

Behavioral health apps will understand your state of mind in some very clever ways. Another company we both work with, Mindstrong, uses artificial intelligence to analyze what you type on your phone's keypad to understand whether you're depressed or manic. Other approaches include using an AI-driven chat bot that periodically asks questions that help reveal a person's mental state. It can be customized to feel like an ally, and will know when to bring in a human to help. Many companies will be built around this always-on mental health space, and data about your mental health will help doctors diagnose your physical health—because the two are connected in ways that will become even more obvious once we are able to start analyzing this rich trove of data.

(During the Covid crisis, latent behavioral health issues ballooned, often with no outlet for quick diagnosis or for psychiatrists or psychologists to see their patients. That deficiency in the system especially hurt the heroes on the front line of healthcare who had to manage high levels of stress and, afterwards, PTSD related to caring for the tsunami of Covid patients.)

While data is fantastically valuable, it will not truly change your health experience if it remains stuck in silos, if every app and healthcare system keeps your data to itself. Each person must be able to own his or her data, and make decisions about what to do with it. Laws and regulations will have to change to make this happen.

The Affordable Care Act, signed by President Obama in 2010, pushed health systems to adopt electronic medical records, and most did—around 96 percent of hospitals in the U.S. now use them. But they were not built to gather, organize and share data—they were built to digitize billing. In other words, like much technology in healthcare, EMRs have been set up to make what healthcare systems already do more efficient. But now dozens of different EMR systems are in use. None of them talk to each other very well. Data in one can't easily be shared with another, though the new federal rules are an attempt to change that. EMRs are so demanding to use that they compound frustration for physicians, which is bad for many reasons. There is ample data showing that physician burnout is partially caused by the degradation of the patient–physician experience and all the extra data entry doctors must do.[3]

We all need a fresh approach here, building on new rules that give patients access to their data. It should work something like your Dropbox account. The data in it is yours. You can get to it, or add to it, anytime. If you want to share all of it with your doctor or a family

---

[3] "Doctors' Suicide Rate Highest of Any Profession," by Pauline Anderson, *WebMD*, May 8, 2018.

member, you can. Or you can decide to share discrete files if you don't think your dentist needs to know about your sleep habits. Thanks to new standards like FHIR, all your health and medical data could flow into one place: your genomic data, microbiome, blood work, data streamed from wearable devices, lab results, MRIs, drug prescriptions, notes from every doctor who sees you. Today, if you switch doctors, you have to beg the old one to send records to the new one. (Imagine if you decided to move your savings account from Wells Fargo to Citibank, and had to go to the head of your local branch to get permission.) When you control your records, all you'll have to do is change a password, or send a link with permissions to the new doctor. The technology would keep track of every person who opens your record, so you'd always know if an unauthorized person looked in. (Emergency rooms could have "skeleton key" software that could open anyone's health data vault. Since your vault tracks who gets in, you'd know if the skeleton key was used improperly.)

Now, what if all these health data mechanisms get built?

This is where the health assurance concept catalyzes. Care will become an always-on proactive way to keep you healthy, as opposed to reactive care once you're sick. The beauty of all that health data is that an artificial intelligence can be built to learn from it and come to understand your health patterns, and compare them with knowledge about health in general.

Let's fast forward to when Steve's Jefferson Health adopts this new health experience. Jefferson could offer a subscription service to a technology-plus-human package that becomes a new first layer of healthcare—a kind of pre-primary care. You'd sign up with Jefferson's service and give it access to your data—both static data (like DNA) and real-time data (heart rate from your Apple Watch, sleep patterns from your Oura ring, etc.). The AI gets a baseline of your health and then watches and learns from your patterns. The technology is running in the background, constantly keeping an eye on your health. If the AI spots something unusual—you're not sleeping, your temperature is up—it might send a text asking some basic questions. Your answers at first go to an AI bot, and perhaps you figure out that not much is wrong—you're just stressed about a big decision at work or have a cold. But if the AI suspects there's something more, it sends the information to a doctor at Jefferson—a doctor who has enough time to talk to you because the AI is handling a lot of the data collection work that used to suck up the doctor's time. The doctor can then get on a video call and do a deeper exploration with you of what's wrong.

On the flip side, if you're worried about something—like a weird pain in your side—you could text the AI or talk to it like you talk to Siri or Alexa. Because the AI has access to your data, it might be able to make a quick judgement about whether you should take a couple of Advil, or get a doctor on video, or rush to the emergency room. For those of you who are already worried about an AI diagnosing patients: AI is just a first point of preventive care and triage, and it will elevate anything troubling to a physician. The goal is to let the technology handle simple stuff so humans can have time to handle the complicated stuff. (In fact, this is a lot like what already happens inside big data centers. AI learns to look for problems and sorts incoming alerts so automated software can field low-level fixes while elevating more difficult problems to human specialists, who now have more time to handle the tough issues.)

Again, the automated part of the "physical" can happen all the time, in real time, without you even being aware. Health data constantly flows in. The AI constantly learns from it. You have a doc in the cloud taking care of you. Startups and progressive health systems are already working to create such an experience.

Then what happens when you want to see a doctor? From the start the experience won't seem like anything you're used to in healthcare. You'll make an appointment online—something like what ZocDoc and similar services offer today. Once you make the appointment, the provider will ask if you need transportation and might send a Lyft or something like Ambulnz, which can pick you up in a van that has an EMT on board or even oxygen tanks. If you seem to have something dangerously contagious, everyone encountering you would know ahead of time and take precautions.

On the day of your appointment, if the doctor is running late, you'll receive a text, like the one airlines send when a flight is delayed. You'll only show up when the doctor is ready to see you. The "waiting room" will become an anachronism, as wasteful as a line of cars at a toll booth in the era of EZPass. Good riddance. It's a dangerous place where you can catch a virus from other sick people.

You'll meet your doctor in a comfortable room, not while sitting on paper pulled off a roll and spread over an examining table. You don't have to take off your clothes, unless there's something you want the doctor to see or the physical examination is needed to confirm an aspect of the ongoing and continuous data. That's because there's no new data to collect—your data record already has everything the doctor needs to know, and it's been delivered ahead of your meeting.

The doctor isn't seeing you to collect data—he or she is seeing you to *talk* to you. The best doctors will act as health coaches and sleuths. They will work with you to help you feel better, or be more productive, or maybe just play better tennis. If something is wrong, they will have the time to dig deep and diagnose it. If you're otherwise well, the physician might ask about your goals for the coming year. Do you want to lose weight before a college reunion? Train for a marathon? Figure out why you're not sleeping? Based on your data, the doctor can help formulate a plan, and set up data-driven goals so you will know if you're staying on track. The doctor becomes the human in the middle as your online data meets your offline physical and mental status.

What else is changing? Well, maybe you need medication. Having all this data makes it far more likely that the physician can prescribe a drug that will be effective for you, without side effects. No need to trudge to a pharmacy, either. The medications will be delivered to you that day—by courier now, but eventually by drone or self-piloting mini robots.

Failure to take medications is one of the chief reasons patients end up back at a doctor's office or emergency room. Soon, pills will contain a tiny ingestible chip that can tell an app whether you're following through. That's not science fiction. Companies like Proteus Digital Health are already in this business.

How will you pay for this new kind of physical? It won't be through insurance. We'll get into this later, but "health insurance" is not insurance at all—it's a perverse, punitive payment system that proved its worthlessness during Covid. The new health experience will work more like a subscription service. Since a great deal of the work is automated by software, the cost can be reasonable, and it can be tiered, like many other services today. An effective but basic version could cost low-income people almost nothing. People with means might pay for a premium version with more features. The business models for such services will be worked out by entrepreneurs, health assurance companies and policymakers.

One of the most important features of health assurance is that prices will be clearly stated. Just like almost everything else in the world, prices for doctors' services, medications, lab tests, online services, medical devices and treatments will be—*must be*—transparent, which is the opposite of healthcare pricing today. Everything in health assurance will be rated and reviewed by users, just like on Airbnb or Amazon. If you need blood pressure medication, you'll be able to shop for the best price. If you need a knee replacement, you'll be able to look at packages from around the world, and decide where to have it done based on prices, ratings, reviews, features, and details about how much time it will take and outcomes for other patients.

"Health insurance" will come to be what insurance is supposed to be: a hedge against risk. Health insurance will cover your care if you run into a tree skiing, or are diagnosed with multiple sclerosis. It won't—and shouldn't—cover simply taking care of your health.

One more thing about the modern, always-on physical: It cannot be a one-size-fits-all model. Instead, it must be built around each individual for that moment—in other words, consumer segmentation. The service for a healthy twenty-something could be built around a general practitioner who acts as a life coach. A mid-30s woman who wants to have children will reorient her service around an ob-gyn or maternity nurse who can guide her through that part of life. If an older person is diagnosed with a chronic condition, the service would be reoriented around that. The AI and data make it possible to profitably tailor health services to each individual. We call this "empathy at scale"—each individual will feel as if the whole medical system is focused on his or her unique health condition.

The innovations and companies to make health assurance a reality are being built right now. The forces driving these changes are too great to be stopped by vested interests or conventional wisdom.

* * *

For entrepreneurs and innovators to understand the opportunities ahead, it might help to understand how the "user experience" in healthcare got to where it is—and why it doesn't have to be that way.

How did the experience become so bad for an industry in which so many people want to do good?

Prior to the 1960s, healthcare in the U.S. was a craft, not an industry. Most doctors worked independently. Many made house-calls. The "family doctor" often knew you from childhood to adulthood—knew you well enough to cater care to you, and knew you well enough to have empathy for you. Doctors and patients built relationships with each other. And healthcare was generally much more straightforward: you called the doctor when you were sick, went to the hospital in an emergency, and otherwise steered clear of both.

Demographics helped force a change. By the 1970s, Baby Boomers were reaching adulthood and having a new wave of children; at the same time, lifespans were lengthening, which steadily increased the elderly population. All these people—especially babies and older people—generated enormous new demand for healthcare. That drove up prices and created scarcity. In order to deliver more care to more people at a reasonable price and profit-margin, healthcare had to become a mass-production affair. It needed economies of scale. And just like in any other business, you achieve economies of scale when you produce the same thing for a lot of people.

This drove mergers, which drove a need for standardized management practices and a push to be more efficient and cut costs. This is how healthcare became an industry. The big hospital mergers started in earnest in the 1990s, then went into warp drive in the 2000s.[4] From 2007 to 2012, according to a Harvard University report, there were 432 hospital mergers in the U.S. involving 835 hospitals. From

---

[4] As detailed in *Unscaled: How AI and a New Generation of Upstarts are Creating the Economy of the Future*, by Hemant Taneja with Kevin Maney, PublicAffairs, 2018.

2004 to 2011, hospital ownership of physician practices increased from 24 percent to 49 percent. By the mid-2010s, 37 percent of hospitals also owned skilled nursing facilities, 62 percent owned hospice services, and 15 percent offered assisted living services. (Steve's Jefferson was part of this trend, with six mergers in five years.) And it wasn't just hospitals that sought scale and integration. By the 2010s, Express Scripts had become an enormous pharmacy benefits manager, processing more than 1.3 billion claims a year, while Labcorp and Quest Diagnostics mushroomed into giants of the testing business. Perversely, new technology that improved care—and we've invented a great deal of amazing tech, from MRI machines to robotic surgeons—became an excuse to raise prices and improve margins.

None of that was good for the experience of people receiving all that care. The drive for ever greater economies of scale worked against the user experience and sapped empathy from practitioners. Standardizing as much as possible made practitioners force patients into existing processes rather than treat them as individuals. The quest for efficiency meant doctors were given strict time-limits when seeing patients, and waiting rooms became packed so not a moment of a doctor's time was wasted. Drug companies invested in medications likely to work for the most people possible, even though an individual needs medication that works best for him or her. Hospitals became monolithic, rigid and impersonal because monolithic, rigid and impersonal was more cost-effective than distributed, flexible and bespoke.

In parallel, another element contributed to the turn away from a good user experience: the rise of insurance to pay for everything in healthcare. It's basically an accident of history.[5] In the 1920s, medi-

---

[5] "Accidents of History Created U.S. Health System," by Alex Blumberg and Adam Davidson, NPR.com, October 22, 2009.

cine was still crude and often ineffective, and most people avoided it. An official at Baylor University Hospital in Dallas, the story goes, noticed that locals spent more on cosmetics than on healthcare. To bring in more customers, the hospital set up a subscription plan for school teachers: pay 50 cents a month, and use the hospital anytime. A few years later, when the Great Depression hit, hospitals across the country saw business plummet. To bring it back, many adopted Baylor's idea. The payment plan came to have a name wherever it was offered: Blue Cross.

The Blue Cross plan was a modest success, but then war engulfed the world. During World War II, the U.S. government set up price and wage controls. Factories were ramping up production for the war effort and needed to attract good people. Since the companies couldn't compete on wages (frozen), they started adding benefits. Employers paid for Blue Cross or other emerging plans like it. By 1943, the government ruled that such benefits should be tax free. As the war ended and the U.S. economy exploded, competition for talent became even more intense, and an employer that didn't offer health benefits risked falling behind. The unemployment rate was just 2.7 percent in 1952, after two years of GDP growth above 8 percent. The combination of events meant that almost everyone worked for a company offering health benefits, and that let the government off the hook. Unlike in other advanced countries, there was no need to set up a national health care system, because private industry was taking care of it. In 1940, just 9 percent of the population had employer-paid health coverage. By the 1960s, it was 70 percent. (By late 2019, the U.S. was in a healthcare coverage crisis because the percentage of Americans covered by employer-based insurance had fallen to 55.7 percent, thanks to cuts in benefits at big companies, higher unemployment, and more people working for small companies that can't afford health plans.

With all the layoffs and business failures amid Covid, insurance coverage has been falling dramatically.)

The spread of health benefits and the vast improvements in medicine combined to do fantastic good in the middle of the twentieth century. The population became healthier and lived longer. Polio, smallpox and measles were nearly eradicated. But as those 1960s and 1970s Boomer-driven demographic changes kicked in, both healthcare systems and insurers needed to grow, standardize, and serve the most people possible. In other words, economics pushed medicine into mass production. It became a factory. The experience for patients became more impersonal, frustrating and costly. Consumers would have complained loudly if another industry had done this, and voted with their wallets to put crappy offerings out of business and reward those that offered better service. But consumers weren't paying for anything—benefits paid for healthcare, so they either didn't have a say, or didn't have to care. With neither the government nor consumers policing the industry and making it behave like most consumer-facing industries, healthcare operated in a bubble, where it could drastically raise prices while giving its customers a worse experience—and, outrageously, develop a system where everyone made more money if people were sicker.

The current system is not some inevitability—it's an accident. And it can be reversed and reinvented.

Today's unscaling forces allow highly-focused companies to profitably deliver personalized, terrific customer experiences, often giving everyday consumers service that used to cost a fortune. An unscaled Uber lets anyone have a car and driver for less than the cost of a taxi. An unscaled Netflix offers a personally-tailored trove of movies for less than the cost of one old-school theater ticket per month. Unscaling is coming to healthcare and it will undo last century's economies of scale. It will usher in a new era of personalized, seamless customer experiences that look nothing like healthcare of the past.

Every time an industry has started to unscale, the dynamic has generated tremendous innovation and company creation. It's healthcare's turn.

* * *

One of our companies, Livongo, is an early example of how healthcare will unscale into health assurance. It also illustrates, in a way we weren't anticipating before Covid, how health assurance can make a society's entire healthcare infrastructure more flexible and resilient.

We discussed earlier what the new health assurance experience might be like for someone who is generally healthy. But medical care takes on a whole different meaning for the millions of people who have chronic conditions. The toll on their lives and on their wallets is far greater. How will health assurance work for them?

In 2014, Hemant and Glen Tullman founded Livongo to help people with diabetes manage the disease. Until then, most innovation around diabetes made users think even more about their condition. Livongo was designed to help people think much less about their conditions. Also, the economies-of-scale healthcare industry has been pulled toward standardizing the way diabetes is treated, so patients are lumped into type 1 and type 2 groups, and those have pretty much the same course of treatment. They see their doctors only occasionally and too often wind up in emergency rooms when their condition goes awry. Livongo's philosophy is that every person's diabetes is unique, so the system must get to know *your* diabetes before it can help you uniquely manage it.

Jefferson Health signed up to try Livongo. Any patient who goes to Jefferson for help with diabetes receives a small mobile device that is both a glucose meter and pedometer (to track exercise). The device connects to the cloud and communicates back to Livongo software. As you check glucose levels, the device sends the data to Livongo and an AI starts to recognize your patterns.

Livongo does not make the old model of diabetes treatment more efficient. It reinvents how diabetes is managed. It doesn't replace a doctor; it gives people with diabetes more power to manage their lives so they need to see doctors less often, and almost never for emergencies. It takes away some of the burden of thinking about diabetes. At Jefferson, we found that people who have diabetes and use Livongo are happier with their experience than those who treat their condition the old-fashioned way. As mentioned earlier, that was Steve's "a-ha! moment," when he realized the power of folding a new, unscaled way of doing things into an existing healthcare infrastructure.

During the worst of the Covid crisis, we saw something interesting from Livongo's users. Hospitals and doctors' offices were filling up with Covid patients. That made going to a hospital or doctor's office both difficult and dangerous. By leaning more heavily on Livongo, many diabetics were able to put off those visits and manage their conditions on their own, which may have saved the lives of people who needed immediate help. In that way, the virtual care of Livongo helped the physical medical infrastructure be more flexible, redirecting diabetic care to take care of Covid patients.

Livongo calls its category of healthcare "applied health signals," and is expanding to help with other chronic conditions such as hypertension and obesity. It's the right way to serve those customers, by organizing care around the condition. (Jefferson and Steve are helping the company develop that model for other conditions, an example of the new way tech entrepreneurs and the traditional healthcare ecosystem can work together earlier in the development process.)

There will be room for many more Livongos in health assurance. Livongo is doing this for the 30 million Americans with diabetes, but other companies will help with all manner of conditions, from depression to erectile dysfunction, addiction, high-risk pregnancy and more. Technology entrepreneurs and healthcare leaders and innovators must come together to reinvent the experience, as Livongo did. They must think about and create opportunities to move healthcare out of the mass-production factory model and into the personalized unscaled model.

All in all, we're seeing that this industry can shift from giving customers an impersonal and frustrating experience to creating experiences consumers love.

3

How Healthcare Can Reinvent Itself... If It's Not Already Too Late

Building health assurance is one of the greatest business opportunities in history. How often in any generation does a multi-trillion-dollar global industry go through a reinvention?

For anyone already in healthcare, the coming decade will be something like being in transportation in the mid-twentieth century, as trains and horses gave way to cars, and then airplanes. Entrepreneurs and innovators had to invent and make not just cars and airplanes but also a massive infrastructure—airports, airlines, roads, gas stations, radios, motor inns, fast-food joints, suburbs. Nobody could've imagined all the possible products and services, and this opened the way for the creation of new giants—General Motors, Boeing, McDonald's—and new fortunes.

The emergence of health assurance will be just as enormous and just as thrilling. Everyone in the healthcare industry will have a chance to help recast "sick care" with a consumer-first mindset and make care better for patients than it has ever been.

Healthcare leaders can embrace this transformation and help drive it—or risk the kind of technology-led disruption that has hollowed out so many other industries. This moment will be to traditional healthcare what the rise of Amazon was to traditional retailers like Sears. Either jump on board, or watch yourself become irrelevant.

As we've discussed, many healthcare systems have been trying to stay afloat by scaling up and merging in order to cut costs and eke out margins while treating patients the same way they've treated patients for decades. But scale is the wrong answer for the 2020s. It will only make the consumer experience more horrible.

Here's a major reason the current system is so bad for consumers, and how it has to change: A health system's customers aren't really the people who come in the door needing medical help. Its customers are the payers—the insurance companies. A doctor or hospital can make a patient happy, yet the insurance company can refuse to pay for that care. The insurance company wants to pay for as little as possible. The math is pretty simple; an insurer wants to take in more money from employers or individuals than it pays out. (There's even a term for that: medical loss ratio.) The result is that no one has a financial incentive to do the best thing for the most important consumer, the patient.

So, an old-style healthcare provider wants to do what insurance will pay for, and the insurance company wants to do as little as possible. No one in that model is properly motivated to do what's best for the person who needs care.

Generally speaking, insurance in the old system paid for procedures, not results. Providers were incentivized to do more tests, more exams, and more surgeries regardless of whether that course of action was best for the consumer. A surgeon who made mistakes and had to do more surgeries to fix the botched attempt could've made more money than a surgeon who always got it right the first time, since insurance paid for each procedure. While some of these upside-down incentives have changed, market forces are still warped. In most normal industries, if you make enough mistakes you go out of business. In healthcare, many can still profit from their poor outcomes.

In order for consumers to make good decisions about their care, they need clear pricing. That rarely happens in old healthcare. Insurance companies negotiate prices with each healthcare provider and don't want to reveal those prices to the public because payers don't want one provider to argue that it should be paid as much as another. Healthcare systems often inflate claims, knowing payers will deny some and pay a fraction of others. The result: consumers don't know what almost anything in healthcare will cost.

Meanwhile, regulations protect hospital finances, allowing them to keep prices artificially high. A hospital can make ten or twenty times more if a patient comes into the emergency room for a minor problem instead of going online and talking to a telehealth doctor, even though most consumers would be better off starting with an online visit.

Many books have been written about how convoluted the U.S. healthcare system is, and how it shields itself from informed consumer choices.[6] Most industries are motivated to please consumers—to give them the best experience at the best price. Otherwise, people will go elsewhere. That market-shaping mechanism has been absent from just about every corner of healthcare.

One result of this consumer-unfriendly approach: the industry has been a target for politicians. Whether on the right or the left, they have painted the industry as bloated, wasteful, overpriced, secretive and monopolistic. Post-Covid, the politicians feel more pressure than ever to fix healthcare, and if the industry doesn't reinvent itself, new health policy might make a bad situation worse.

---

[6] We recommend David Goldhill's *Catastrophic Care: Why Everything We Think We Know about Health Care Is Wrong*, Vintage Publishing, 2013.

At the same time, frustrated industry constituents—providers, employers, insurers, governments, patients—are also trying to force change, first by blaming every other constituent in the complex healthcare ecosystem, and then by trying to shift costs onto those other constituents. Healthcare analyst Paul Keckley put it this way in one of his newsletters: "In addressing healthcare affordability, as an industry, we're prone to circle the wagons and shoot in. It's sector vs. sector combat. Each asserts its own efforts to cut costs and increase price transparency. Each accuses others of wastefulness and ill-gotten gain. Each points to complicating factors—some legitimate and some not—to counter criticism. That's the state of play: each sector protecting its own interest." [7]

This "who's gonna take the blame" mentality of the current healthcare system will only get worse in the aftermath of Covid, with more uninsured and under-employed people in this country than any time since the Great Depression. At the same time, insurers, providers and payers will try to make up for lost income and the easy path will be doubling down on the sick-care system. If they're smart, consumers, business leaders and policymakers will not take it anymore and accelerate the drive toward this new system.

All of these misaligned incentives have helped create the opportunity to reinvent healthcare into health assurance. In late-2019, we would've said that because the system is so large, complex and regulated, change won't happen in a flash—that it won't be "disrupted" the way Uber upended taxis in a few years. But after Covid, we're not so sure. All bets are off.

---

[7] "Healthcare Affordability: The Two Urgent Imperatives," *The Keckley Report*, August 5, 2019. https://www.paulkeckley.com/the-keckley-report/2019/8/5/healthcare-affordability-the-two-urgent-imperatives

So if you're a leader or professional in healthcare today, you can struggle with internecine warfare, bad political solutions and a slow-motion collapse as costs drive away customers. Or you can grab this opportunity and contribute to the emergence of a consumer-centric health assurance industry that will be a vast improvement.

* * *

For years, smart people in healthcare have known the industry should put patients in the center. That has been the topic of countless research reports, board meetings and industry conferences. While it seems like a radical idea, it just means that the healthcare industry must operate more like nearly every other consumer-facing industry.

A handful of health systems have been trying—and showing it's possible for incumbents to find new ways of doing business. Kaiser Permanente is both an insurance company and a healthcare provider for its plan members, so that eliminates some of the perverse economics and creates more incentive for Kaiser to do what's cost-effective for consumers. For its 4.4 million plan members in northern California, Kaiser started offering options to connect with doctors via phone, email or video. Eighty-seven percent of members said video visits were more convenient than showing up in person, and 84 percent said a digital office visit improved their relationship with their physician. "Members seem to be saying, 'I use FaceTime with my daughter or video-conference at work, so I can do a video visit with my doctor,'" says Mary Reed, an official at Kaiser Permanente Northern California.[8] In

---

[8] "Kaiser patients give a thumbs up to digital visits," Mark Brohan, *Internet Health Management*, June 22, 2019. https://www.digitalcommerce360.com/2019/07/22/kaiser-patients-give-a-thumbs-up-to-digital-visits/

other words, Kaiser found that patients like the convenient way they interact with most other kinds of companies.

At Intermountain Healthcare, a Salt Lake City-based system of 24 hospitals and 160 clinics, CEO Marc Harrison has been trying to drive a shift to digital, consumer-first healthcare, even though it sometimes has meant cannibalizing revenue and changing the way people get care. "You'll get a lot of crap as you disrupt—angry calls from doctors, the community, the state legislature," Harrison said, before Covid. "You have to be willing to suffer to make this kind of change."[9] Intermountain, for instance, started a subscription-based primary care service, often called direct primary care. By mid-2020, Intermountain expects to have shifted 100,000 patients to that model, which aims to keep people healthy instead of just treating them when sick. Those who use the service, Harrison said, have a 60 percent reduction in hospital visits. In other words, the service eats away at one of the ways a system like Intermountain traditionally makes most of its money. However, when a catastrophe like Covid strikes, such a service frees up resources for the critically ill. That's one way Covid illuminated a benefit of moving a traditional system to health assurance.

At Jefferson, we have a similar offering called JeffConnect for our employees, instituted well before Covid. We're both the payer (as a self-insured employer) and the provider (as a healthcare system) for that population, which helps align us better with consumers (i.e., our employees). If our employees check out a medical problem by telehealth using JeffConnect, we waive the deductible, even if we direct them to one of our emergency rooms. If they show up at the ER without going through virtual triage, there is a starting deductible of $500. That one change has made for happier patients (they get care closer

---

[9] Interview with Marc Harrison by Kevin Maney, October 2019.

to home through tele-health, urgent care or a doctor's office), and has reduced Jefferson's unscheduled care costs by 25 percent. So, when our people use JeffConnect, they save time and money and we, the employer, save time and money. Everyone is happier.

Such examples are rare in traditional healthcare. The industry needs some leaders who will break the mold, embrace new ways of serving consumers, and help us stay healthy and out of doctor's offices and hospitals. What most consumers really want is as little healthcare as possible.

Some new companies are showing how consumer-centric health assurance can work. Established healthcare systems would do well to partner with such startups, invest in them, or at least learn from them.

One company offering consumer-centric health assurance is Ro, the company behind sites such as Roman and Rory. Ro offers an easy experience for people who want to treat conditions like erectile dysfunction and insomnia. You can see prices and products; communicate with a doctor online; get a prescription; order the drugs; and have them delivered to your door in slick packaging that would make Apple proud. The cost and time commitment for consumers is a fraction of going to a doctor's office (and sitting for lord-knows-how-long in a waiting room), taking a prescription to a pharmacy (and waiting in line), and only finding out how much the drugs will cost once the pharmacist rings up the order. This kind of service is enjoying a ton of press coverage and traction with consumers. Investors (including Hemant's firm) pumped nearly $100 million in funding into Ro by mid-2019.

Ro can operate in a consumer-friendly way because it goes around the traditional healthcare system. It doesn't take insurance or prescriptions from your doctor, yet is making these medications more affordable for most people. It's showing that if consumers find a cheap, easy and transparent way to treat a problem, many will choose that route even if they have health insurance. The gap between a good consumer experience and the usual experience in healthcare is that great.

Livongo, as described in the previous chapter, is showing what the consumer-centric health assurance approach can do for people with chronic conditions. In a typical healthcare setting, if you're diagnosed with a chronic condition, you're pretty much left to manage it on your own. You have to find a doctor, make appointments, get the right medications and take them, learn ways to live that lower the impact of the condition, and on and on. There is no hub, no quarterback, to help you.

The idea behind Livongo is that technology in conjunction with healthcare professionals can act as that hub, that quarterback. It puts the patient at the center, and organizes the care around his or her unique condition and circumstances. The service can guide the patient's lifestyle choices and track use of medications. It can tell the patient when to see a doctor and when to do something simple to feel better. These kinds of services allow the patient to think less and do less about his or her chronic condition.

For consumers who are generally healthy, healthcare systems have an opportunity to build what we call virtual primary care. To see how this might work, look at companies like Forward, which pitches itself as membership-based, data-driven "continuous primary care." In New York City, for instance, you pay $149 a month for a kind of always-on family doctor. There are doctors in an office, and you can see one as often as you want. When you sign up, you get a genetic test and blood test to start building data about your body and health. There's a Forward app that monitors sleep, exercise and other vital signs, and adds the data to your record. In March 2020, Forward added a Covid risk assessment to its app, helping its users navigate the pandemic and know when to see a doctor. A chat bot is available any time, so if you wake up at 2 a.m. with a fever, you can start a chat; if the software realizes you might have a dangerous flu or, say, appendicitis, it will alert a live medical professional to intervene or send you to a hospital.

Like Ro and Livongo, Forward works outside the old system. It doesn't take insurance, but is counting on winning over consumers by offering a great experience at a good value. When you factor in copays and deductibles, using direct primary care could save money for a lot of consumers.

Forward was started in 2017 by Adrian Aoun, a former Google executive who oversaw the launch of Alphabet's Sidewalk Labs. He's not a healthcare insider, but he has big plans that healthcare systems might want to pay attention to. "We want to build the world's biggest healthcare system," Aoun told *Business Insider*. "We're planning on launching more and more services until one day we're able to perform open heart surgery." [10]

Why wouldn't a healthcare system build something like this? Or why not partner with a company like Forward to give consumers virtualized, always-on primary care that then connects to the system's hospitals and specialists for emergencies and acute medical problems?

Forward is trying to create a complete healthcare experience. By charging a flat fee, it is banking on keeping people healthier so they don't have to visit high-cost human doctors. The software and services and coaching are relatively cheap to offer at scale. Plus, if fewer of its members need to see doctors, those doctors will have more time for

---

[10] "This ex-Googler helped reimagine what cities could look like—now his new startup, Forward, is using tech to rethink healthcare," by Zoe Bernard, *Business Insider*, November 24, 2018.https://www.businessinsider.com/forward-new-york-city-healthcare-2018-11

people who do come in. The company doesn't make money on sick care—it makes money on keeping its members as healthy as possible.

We see offerings like Ro, Livongo and Forward as just the beginning, and believe there are even greater opportunities for health professionals who put consumers first.

For instance, the industry has rarely even considered consumer segmentation, the way many brands do. Think of how different consumer segments might be attracted to services geared for them. Imagine a version of Forward for people over 70, aimed at helping them stay healthy as they age. Or a version for pregnant women, with an OB/GYN doctor at the center instead of a family practitioner. Or a version for young athletes whose goal is to stay as physically fit as possible. And in each of those categories, there's an opening to offer different levels of care, from basic to super-premium. Perhaps you'd pay more for "all-you-can-eat" access and less for restricted access. Almost every kind of health assurance service could be tweaked for specific consumer segments. As care becomes more virtualized, companies will be able to profitably cater to ever narrower segments.

This is the core of unscaling. Companies are taking apart the scaled-up, mass-market operations of last century and replacing them with highly-focused, profitable niche offerings that better serve consumers in that segment. If a consumer can get a customized health experience through the cloud that feels like it was made just for him or her, why would that person ever walk into a mass-market, factory-like general hospital?

* * *

We're not saying a transition to consumer-centric health assurance will be easy for health professionals. Remember that Steve runs a big health system, and understands the challenges. At Jefferson, he has been trying to straddle the line between the past and future. To stay viable, Jefferson has had to operate like a typical healthcare system—the strategy has been to scale up, drive efficiencies, become even more one-size-fits-all, and be financially sound enough to try new products and services that might make less money now but carry Jefferson into the "healthcare with no address" future later. The Covid crisis convinced Steve of the benefits of this strategy. Jefferson's scale and geographic reach, plus its stable balance sheet, allowed Jefferson to leverage the power of the entire enterprise, move personal protective equipment and ventilators to the most affected hospitals, and keep a few hospitals as non-Covid elective surgery hospitals so that they could take in patients after the surge. The flexibility helped Jefferson stay financially liquid and maintain its 35,000-person workforce in the near term.

At the same time, Jefferson's moves toward health assurance meant it could ramp up telehealth through JeffConnect. Patients who had been accustomed to seeing physicians at other hospitals started using JeffConnect because of its ease of use and then continued as Jefferson patients once the first pandemic spike passed.

Steve's Jefferson and Hemant's General Catalyst are increasingly working together. Jefferson can be a testing ground for new companies that General Catalyst funds, helping those startups see if they'll fly in the real world, and helping the healthcare system learn how to embrace and adapt to these new entities. General Catalyst is tapping Jefferson to advise—and, in some cases, co-invest in—health assurance startups. A next step is to embed Silicon Valley engineers into Jefferson's system, and Jefferson people into General Catalyst's environment. We believe this kind of cooperation is important. The reinvention of healthcare is too complex for any one piece to go it alone.

As the transition takes hold, traditional healthcare leaders will have to think about their business in new ways. Once consumers are spending *their* money on health, prices will fall drastically—and so will administrative costs. A study by healthcare journal *Health Affairs* found that 23.5 percent of healthcare costs are administrative, which leaves a lot of room for savings.[11]

By offering great experiences, health assurance companies will be able to earn customer loyalty. Few hospitals today have that.

By offering services through the cloud, health systems may be able to compete beyond geographic borders, the way Amazon virtualized retail and can compete against any physical store anywhere. That could do wonders for resiliency in a crisis like Covid, allowing hospitals in a less-impacted area to virtually help hospitals being hammered.

The concept of health assurance expands the definition of healthcare beyond wellness, offering chances to engage with consumers about food, exercise, lifestyle and mental well-being—all new business opportunities for much of the industry.

Imagine lifting the burden of administering the 10,000-plus codes now used to track billing of medical procedures. Data collected about patients will become much more useful. Today, the data that goes into most electronic medical records revolves around billing for insurance, which makes it almost useless when it comes to understanding patients and how to better treat them. Take away the labyrinthine billing practices, and the data collected can bring a health system closer to its customers.

In the change from sick care to health assurance, leaders will have

---

[11] "A Comparison of Hospital Administrative Costs In Eight Nations: US Costs Exceed All Others By Far," by David U. Himmelstein, Miraya Jun, Reinhard Busse, Karine Chevreul, Alexander Geissler, Patrick Jeurissen, Sarah Thomson, Marie-Amelie Vinet, Steffie Woolhandler, *Health Affairs*, Vol. 33, No. 9.

to think differently about their workforce. Vastly fewer administration bureaucrats will be needed, but health systems will need to ramp up hiring in customer service, marketing and branding—not to mention technologists, such as software coders and software engineers and user-experience experts.

Consumer-centric health assurance will drive up demand for a new breed of doctor. Today, medical schools are filled with people who are great at memorization. In the dawning age of AI virtual assistants on smartphones in everyone's pocket, memorized knowledge becomes less important than the very human capabilities of empathy, creativity, grace under pressure and communication. The old insurance model has driven the best students to the highest-grossing revenue types of medicine, like dermatology, radiology, orthopedics and anesthesiology. As the new model gets away from paying for procedures and evolves into paying for keeping people healthy, the most valuable doctors will be family physicians and pediatricians. Every forward-thinking medical school should start recruiting these new era medical students now.

One last great challenge for healthcare incumbents will be embracing new beliefs. Health isn't just about medicine; it includes all aspects of life—food, sleep, exercise, mental health, financial situation, geography. The best way to treat any illness is to treat the whole patient. The industry must also accept that a doctor on video—or maybe even an AI-driven chat bot—can diagnose a ruptured appendix as well as a doctor in an emergency room.

The health assurance industry will have to allow consumers more power and responsibility when it comes to their health. A lot of consumers will welcome this shift and refuse to tolerate rotten experiences. Some won't, probably because the current players have convinced them that any other way of providing care will be a health risk.

Powerhouse players in an old industry rarely change in time to stay on top in a new era. But health professionals must play a significant role, and must embrace the idea that a shift to health assurance will be better for all of us. Providers will see lower costs, higher margins, better outcomes and more consumer loyalty. Employers will see the cost of taking care of their people go down for the first time in decades, while the well-being of their employees improves. Consumers will get the help they need to stay healthier longer, and will find that healthcare will eat up less of their hard-earned money.

The sectors that should worry the most about this transformation:

- Hospital systems can't continue to believe they will survive by doing more procedures and only caring for those who show up to their hospitals, doctor's offices or emergency departments. As health assurance takes hold, that kind of operation will come to seem like the post office in the age of email.

- Big pharmaceutical companies will run into trouble if they believe they can continue to charge more for drugs and erect barriers and obfuscations to protect their opaque pricing. As health assurance makes care virtual and global, consumers will force clear, competitive pricing so that choosing a drug is as straightforward as choosing sneakers on Amazon.

- Insurance companies, which have traditionally served as middlemen, now take a cut of transactions and act as a barrier to direct communication between the employer, patient and provider. It's such middlemen that get hurt most when markets go digital.

And that leads us into the next chapter...

4

The Case Against Health Insurance as We Know It

Health insurance companies, government insurers like Medicare, and self-insured businesses have had a tough job. They wedged themselves between consumers and healthcare providers. They have to tell consumers what they can and can't do to take care of their health, and as a result add uncertainty and confusion to any patient's life. On the other side, these payers have to tell medical professionals what they can and can't do to treat patients, and what they can charge to do those things—adding bureaucracy and frustration to their work.

We as consumers feel that health insurers don't make decisions with our best interests in mind. Doctors feel insurers don't make decisions with either the doctor's or their patient's best interests in mind.

So, in America, pretty much everyone who doesn't work at a health insurance company scorns health insurance companies. The American Customer Satisfaction Index identifies health insurers as the fourth most-disliked industry in the nation.[12] The only industries

---

[12] "The Top 5 Industries Most Hated by Consumers," by Blake Morgan, *Forbes*, October 16, 2018.

faring worse are cable companies, internet service providers and cell phone service providers. Yet most of the population puts up with what we all know as health insurance. About 60 percent of the population is covered by employer-based insurance, followed by Medicaid (20 percent), Medicare (16 percent), direct-purchase (16 percent) and military coverage (4.7 percent).[13]

To add some cruel irony to this scenario, health insurers are rewarded for making millions of people miserable by making enormous amounts of money.[14] From 2010 to 2019, UnitedHealth, the largest health insurer, tripled its stock price and boosted its net income by 131 percent. Other huge insurers, such as Anthem and Aetna (now CVS Health), saw their stocks triple in value. In April 2020, *Modern Healthcare* reported that health insurer CEOs saw significant pay bumps in 2019—the CEOs of the four largest insurers made around $100 million in total compensation.[15] (The same week, Beckers Hospital Review reported that Mayo Clinic had to furlough or cut hours of 30,000 employees to help offset $3 billion in losses due to the pandemic.)[16]

And where were insurers during Covid? On the surface, some seemed to be trying to help. Cigna, Humana and CVS (Aetna) waived

---

[13] "Census Bureau: 118,395,000 on 'Government Health Insurance' in 2015; 28,966,000 Uninsured for Entire Year," by Terence B. Jeffrey, CNSNews.com, September 13, 2016.

[14] "Obamacare Has Engorged Health Insurer Profits, But That May Change Soon," by Robert Kientz, *Seeking Alpha*, July 30, 2019.

[15] "Health insurer CEOs saw pay bumps in 2019," by Shelby Livingston, *Modern Healthcare*, April 21, 2020.

[16] "Mayo Clinic furloughs, cuts hours of 30,000 employees to help offset $3B in pandemic losses," by Ali Paavola, *Beckers Hospital Review*, April 23, 2020. https://www.beckershospitalreview.com/finance/mayo-clinic-furloughs-cuts-hours-of-30-000-employees-to-help-offset-3b-in-pandemic-losses.html

deductibles and some other costs for customers who had to be hospitalized for Covid-19.[17] But underneath, insurers were making a ton of money. They kept collecting premiums, of course, and had to pay hospitals for Covid patients' care, but the Covid costs were more than offset by a sharp decline in more expensive elective surgeries and other procedures ranging from dermatologist visits to physical therapy. In mid-April, United Healthcare, one of the largest U.S. insurers, reported a three percent increase in first-quarter earnings. In the month before that announcement, its stock had risen 32 percent, from $220 a share to $290. Just a couple weeks earlier, a report from California's insurance marketplace said that insurers are likely to raise premiums as much as 40 percent in 2021, using Covid costs as an excuse.[18]

How does a business like this even exist, much less thrive? And how can entrepreneurs and innovators make things better?

The problem with insurance starts with a unique distortion of the way consumer markets are supposed to work. In most market sectors, the person who decides what to buy, the person who pays for it, and the person who benefits from it are the same: i.e., the consumer. If you go buy a car, you decide which car based on its features, your needs and your budget. You pay for it with your cash or a loan. And then you benefit from it—you get to drive the car.

In healthcare, who decides, who pays and who benefits are all different.

---

[17] "Some Insurers Waive Patients' Share Of Costs For COVID-19 Treatment," by Selena Simmons-Duffin, NPR, March 30, 2020. https://www.npr.org/sections/health-shots/2020/03/30/824075753/good-news-with-caveats-some-insurers-waive-costs-to-patients-for-covid-19-treatm.

[18] "Coronavirus May Add Billions to U.S. Health Care Bill," by Reed Abelson, *The New York Times*, March 28, 2020. https://www.nytimes.com/2020/03/28/health/coronavirus-insurance-premium-increases.html

If you have chest pains and rush to a hospital, a medical professional decides what to do. You most likely have little input—no way to make a choice based on likely outcomes and your budget. A third party—an insurance company—will pay for it, so there's no discussion of costs between you and the hospital. Neither you nor the doctor knows what you'll ultimately be charged or what the doctor or hospital will make. Yet it's you who benefits from the care, even though you've had almost no input on what you're buying or how much you're paying.

Separating those three elements—deciding, paying, benefiting— results in strange behaviors in the market. Insurance companies set negotiated prices with health systems for almost everything, and the financial incentive for insurers is to pay out as little as possible while charging policyholders as much as possible. Consumers have no good way to find the best care for the best price because the negotiated prices are mostly secret. And since insurance often feels like someone else's money, consumers don't have much incentive to shop on price. And since the consumer isn't paying, many health providers look for ways to charge insurance companies as much as possible, so they add tests and follow-up visits and other actions that might be overkill but have an insurance billing code.

Prices have nothing to do with supply and demand, or quality, or customer satisfaction. All the consumer-driven checks and balances that motivate other companies in other industries to offer a competitive product at a competitive price are messed up in healthcare.

Insurers can charge consumers ever more while delivering ever less, and squeeze healthcare systems on price. (That's why insurance company stock prices have tripled.)

The good news in all this bad news is that this perversion of the market is creating opportunities. New kinds of software-driven companies are starting to change how we buy and pay for healthcare, and that shift will eat away at insurers the way Netflix and Hulu have been gnawing on cable TV. The post-Covid economic downturn is amplifying the opportunity by tossing so many Americans off their health insurance. As of this writing, more than 22 million people had filed for unemployment, and a lot of those workers no doubt lost health insurance when they lost their jobs. So we are at a moment in time when a surge of people will need insurance and may be open to alternatives to the incumbents.

The key for entrepreneurs and innovators who want to take advantage of this opportunity is to reassemble the consumer mechanism of deciding, paying and benefiting. Aligning those changes everything in healthcare.

* * *

If you sign up for one of Ro's services—perhaps to manage erectile dysfunction, or menopause, or hypertension—no part of it involves insurance. You answer some questions online, consult with a doctor online, request a prescription online, choose the clearly-priced drug to buy online, pay online with a credit card, and have the drugs delivered to your mailbox on a monthly schedule. You (the consumer) decide, pay, and benefit. That drives Ro to build a great user experience at a good price—if it doesn't, another company will, and you'll go there instead.

Ro is an unscaled company. A consumer with erectile dysfunction feels as though Ro is focused directly at him, making for an experience that's better than going into the office of a doctor who treats every kind of condition. The absence of insurance helps Ro make everything simple, and gives power back to the consumer. You decide, you pay, you benefit.

Livongo is also outside the insurance-driven norm. The consumer decides whether to use it, and the consumer benefits from it. Consumers are choosing Livongo even if they have insurance because it makes them healthier, so their care costs less. By aligning who decides, pays and benefits, Livongo is teaching consumers to not depend solely on health insurers and hospitals. That's allowed Livongo to build a multi-billion-dollar chronic illness management service in just five years.

Companies like Ro and Livongo show how health assurance—keeping people healthy instead of just treating them when sick—can reshape the economics of healthcare. These companies use technology to offer great experiences for specific needs, peeling off pieces of the traditional mass-market, everything-to-everybody approach of hospital systems and insurance companies. The newcomers reassemble the broken formula of consumer markets, so consumers decide, pay and benefit. The result is an offering that is user-friendly, convenient, cost-effective, and relentlessly competitive.

Most traditional healthcare is heading in the opposite direction. Look at the mergers that made headlines in recent years. Drugstore giant CVS merged with insurer Aetna in a $70-billion deal. CVS Health CEO Larry Merlo said he wants to create a "new front door to healthcare"—apparently so your insurance can guide you to CVS clinics and pharmacies, creating efficiencies and cutting costs by keeping everything under one corporate roof. It remains to be seen how much of that new "health hub" strategy is aimed at transforming the consumer experience.[19] Health insurer Cigna and pharmacy ben-

---

[19] "We asked the CEO of CVS to share how he plans to use his 10,000 pharmacies to upend healthcare. This is the story he told us," by Lydia Ramsey, *Business Insider*, Nov 8, 2019. https://www.businessinsider.com/cvs-health-ceo-larry-merlo-on-how-healthhubs-are-working-2019-11

efit managing group Express Scripts merged in 2018 in a $71-billion deal. Again, the merger is mostly about driving economies of scale to save costs for the companies.[20]

The quest for economies of scale infects every part of the industry. Insurance companies have been trying to run healthcare systems. Some insurers have offered to partner with Jefferson to use their experience managing back office functions, revenue cycles and supply chain, and promise increased profits. Jefferson would essentially become a real estate company, managing healthcare buildings and leaving the rest to the insurer. But that wouldn't benefit the consumer.

Employers, frustrated with the rising costs of health benefits, have been trying to build their own networks of insurance and healthcare for employees. The most notable attempt is Haven, which is being created by Amazon, JPMorgan Chase and Berkshire Hathaway. While Haven is still unproven, its purpose seems to be to save money, not improve experiences. As Warren Buffett, Berkshire's CEO, said when Haven was unveiled, health care costs are "a hungry tapeworm on the American economy." That's a need-to-cut-costs perspective, not a make-a-better-experience point of view.[21]

All these cost-saving strategies reflect a last-century way of thinking: combine forces, grow, gain economies of scale, automate as much as possible, put in processes to create efficiencies, and give the same kind of mass-market care to as many people as possible. They are doubling down on making healthcare even more of an impersonal black box that costs too much and is a crappy experience for everyone. That makes these companies more vulnerable to unscaled

---

[20] "Five Takeaways About Cigna's Strategy for Express Scripts," *Drug Channels*, March 27, 2018.

[21] "Amazon, Berkshire Hathaway And JPMorgan Chase Launch New Health Care Company," by Bill Chappell and Colin Dwyer, NPR.com, January 30, 2018.

disruptors. A large-scale, impersonal, expensive, mass-market experience will always lose to an unscaled, personalized, money-saving, user-friendly experience.

* * *

Until recently, most healthcare startups had to hope insurance would pay for whatever they were selling. If consumers couldn't get something covered by insurance, the thinking went, then they wouldn't buy it. But consumers are already responding differently, replacing insurance-driven decisions with consumer-driven decisions.

From a consumer standpoint, insurance plans are looking more like self-pay plans. As many of us know, employers for years have been pushing more of the burden of paying for health insurance onto employees.

Almost all of the burden of rising health insurance and healthcare costs are shifted to the employee—because employers are paying healthcare costs instead of giving raises. As David Goldhill points out in his book, *Catastrophic Health Care*, studies show that, "the bulk of growth in compensation costs in the decade 1996–2006 went to employer health premiums; in other words, spending on health insurance crowded out growth in wages. Wages could actually decline over time to compensate for higher employer health costs."[22]

As insurance costs have rocketed, strapped consumers (or their employers) have chosen plans with ever-higher deductibles. That essentially means the consumer pays out of pocket for everything but critical problems. Paying out of pocket forces consumers to think more rationally about medical care—they are motivated to look for

---

[22] *Catastrophic Care*, by David Goldhill, pg. 64, Vintage, 2013.

good experiences at competitive prices. More and more, millions of insured workers are shopping for healthcare the way they'd shop for a car. They are returning to the deciding/paying/benefiting formula.

At the same time, the high cost of insurance was already causing it to be abandoned by two ends of the market: low-income and high-income individuals.

In January 2020, the Gallup National Health and Well-Being Index reported that the percentage of adults without health insurance was 13.7 percent, up from 10.9 percent just two years earlier.[23] For households with income less than $24,000, the rate rose to 25.4 percent from 22.6 percent two years prior. All those numbers are certainly higher now, with the massive unemployment caused by Covid lockdowns. When uninsured, low-income consumers pay for healthcare, they are extremely price-sensitive. That opens up opportunities. Goldhill, the author cited above, co-founded a company called Sesame that lets healthcare professionals advertise specials much the way a grocery store would post sales: MRI for $149, down from $500; physical therapy for $19, down from $159. The fact that Sesame exists shows there's been a shift in consumer thinking.

High-income consumers are less concerned about costs but want to buy a better experience. Many wealthy individuals are opting for a high-deductible insurance plan that would kick in if, for instance, they crashed into a tree skiing. But they are skipping insurance for routine care. Instead, many pay for primary-care doctors and medical concierge services that don't take insurance and promise great customer service. In other words, for several thousand dollars a year, you can get the kind of care you used to expect from every doctor. "Direct primary care" practices are taking off. They often charge a

---

[23] "Gallup Reports 4-Year High in Number of Uninsured Americans," by Kyle Murphy, *Health Payer Intelligence*, January 25, 2019.

flat monthly fee and allow customers to see a doctor as often as they want. The American Academy of Family Physicians reports that in 2019 there were more than 1,000 direct primary care practices in the U.S., up from about 125 in 2014.[24] We anticipate that Covid will accelerate this trend.

As more people stop relying on insurance to pay for everything, that will increase demand for consumer-friendly services. As entrepreneurs and innovators see those opportunities, they'll build more companies and offerings that deliver great experiences at competitive prices... which in turn will convince more consumers to give up insurance and use new health assurance products and services, generating yet more opportunities for new companies. In other words, build health assurance, and they will come. In fact, they're already on their way.

In a world where insurance-driven decisions fade—when who decides, pays and benefits are the same person—the concept that makes the most economic sense is health assurance. A consumer who moves to health assurance will stay healthier, manage conditions better, see doctors less often, get fewer tests, buy fewer drugs, and spend less overall on their health than they do today.

With health assurance, certain categories will move out of the existing system. People with diabetes, mental health issues, hypertension and other conditions will rely on digital offerings that reduce the number of touch points with the existing system. Nobody has to wait and hope insurers will start covering these offerings—it won't matter. And nobody will have to wait for policymakers to pass health care legislation. *These shifts are happening already.*

And as these shifts happen, they enable the free market to do

---

[24] "A Growing Number of Doctors Take Only Cash, Not Insurance," by Dave Roos, *HowStuffWorks*, August 21, 2019.

what free markets do in other consumer sectors, whether it be cars, computers or golf clubs: drive competitors to build ever-better offerings for attractive prices.

Something else interesting will kick in as patients act more like consumers—staying healthy will become a major financial asset. Sure, your company might give you a few bucks today if you have a gym membership. But if health assurance can keep people healthy and out of the existing system as long as possible, and consumers stop relying on insurance to pay medical bills, many families could save thousands of dollars a year.

* * *

If you put it all together, here's how the financial side of health assurance will likely work. In the next few years, if there are no major policy changes by the federal government, more consumers will choose a low-cost, high-deductible policy meant to cover catastrophic health problems. For routine or predictable needs—even including something like a knee replacement or childbirth—consumers will increasingly choose to opt out of the traditional system and pay out of pocket.

That may seem scary at first, but as more health assurance companies emerge, consumers will be able to find a better experience at lower cost. A company called Nuvo, for instance, aims to take pregnancy and childbirth out of the old system and give expectant mothers a better experience by using data, software and direct-pay clinics at a fraction of what a traditional hospital would charge. (And why would a young, healthy pregnant patient think it's a good idea, post-pandemic, to drive to a hospital full of sick people for monitoring when she could do that at home? Providers not offering such an alternative will be at a significant disadvantage.)

For something like a knee replacement, services will sprout up that can help you find a high-quality surgical center anywhere in the world. Narayana Health, a hospital company in India, has some of the best outcomes and lowest error rates in the world, not to mention luxurious rooms in its premium wing—yet Narayana charges a fraction of what a U.S. hospital would charge for the same procedure.[25] A pulmonary thromboendarterectomy could cost $200,000 in the U.S., but $10,000 at Narayana. (If your insurance has a 20 percent copay, you'd save $30,000 by going to Narayan.) Once you're free from having insurers decide where you have surgery, you can go anywhere based on the cost, outcomes and quality that you want.

We hope laws will change to allow employers to alter the way they think about health benefits. Instead of being forced to offer traditional insurance, we believe employers should be able to offer a healthcare allowance so employees can decide how to spend money on health—according to the deciding/paying/benefiting formula. Perhaps employers would offer a combination of a high-deductible plan to guard against crises that might tip an employee into bankruptcy, along with an allowance for health assurance services.

If the allowance not spent is allowed to roll over year after year, good health becomes a financial asset. Health allowance dollars would pile up as the employee stays healthy, year after year. Assuming the allowance is forfeited if the employee leaves the company, it becomes a retention tool. It would be harder for someone to leave after building up $100,000 in health allowance.

So let's say you have a budget for everyday health and insurance

---

[25] "The World's Cheapest Hospital Has to Get Even Cheaper," by Ari Altstedter, *Bloomberg Businessweek*, March 26, 2019.

for catastrophes. What next? If you're generally healthy, you'll probably become a member of a primary care service, paying a monthly fee for a care package designed to keep you healthy, handle minor problems and act as your health care quarterback if you need more complex care.

People who have an ongoing medical condition—whether diabetes, depression, multiple sclerosis or age-related issues—will subscribe to a primary care service organized around that condition. The service will be a lot like a general primary care service, but will be staffed by professionals who focus on that condition.

A lot of companies will compete to offer you this service. New York-based insurance startup Oscar sees such services as key to its future (or any health insurer's future). Oscar CEO Mario Schlosser reasons that his company will have health records and other data about each customer, and also have connections to health systems and professionals, so it would be in a perfect position to act as a consumer's healthcare quarterback. "If members of Oscar realize from the beginning that if they need a doctor, if they need help, they can come to Oscar first—they can go and search in the app, they can talk to their concierge team, they can use us to make appointments, and we will take care of all of that," Schlosser told *Wired* magazine. "As an insurance company, we already have a lot more data than anybody else in the system." [26]

Primary care services can't handle everything, of course. Almost everyone will need some costly critical care at some point. Maybe it's that skiing accident, or cancer, or a stroke. That's when insurance kicks in—and when you want to abandon that deciding/paying/benefiting

---

[26] "Health Care Is Broken. Oscar Health Thinks Tech Can Fix It," by Nicholas Thompson, *Wired*, August 14, 2018.

formula. If you're in an emergency room after that skiing accident and you have brain trauma, you want a pro to decide what to do, and you don't want to have to calculate how much it will cost. This critical care end of healthcare will likely work much as it does today.

Also, people often need to see specialists. But let's say you need arthroscopic knee surgery, and you plan to pay for it with a health allowance from your company, or pay for it out of pocket. You'll want to be able to shop, balancing price with quality. For that to work, the medical industry must change the way it bills patients, making prices transparent and allowing doctors and surgical centers to be rated and reviewed. You'll want to be able to shop for knee surgery the way you shop for a flight online. The competition for patients will drive prices down and quality up. Although it might sound scary to start paying for surgeries instead of relying on insurance, in a health assurance environment you will save money and get better results.

For entrepreneurs, helping health providers move into a world of transparency and competition will open up vast opportunities. The industry will need software to handle this kind of billing (it's completely different from insurance-style billing), rating systems, and applications that are yet to be imagined.

Does that whole scenario seem far-fetched? It's not. The industry is already moving that way—slowly before Covid, and now accelerating post-Covid. We are at a tipping point.

Covid revealed something else about insurance—or, more accurately, about the ability of everyone to access care. Covid reminded us that our individual health is closely tied to societal health. Keeping the pandemic at bay means testing, diagnosing and treating rich, poor and everyone in the middle. If low-income people can't afford care and aren't checked out when they get sick, it puts everyone else in danger. For the good of all, we need a system that keeps everyone healthy.

But that doesn't necessarily mean "Medicare for all." Senator Bernie Sanders' definition of the problem was correct: we have a healthcare system that does not work for much of the population. But his solution would have the government pay for and entrench the current healthcare system. That would just perpetuate the breaks between who decides, who pays and who benefits. It would cement the healthcare industry as is, in its twentieth-century mindset, and curtail innovation and competition.

As Goldhill has said to us: Medicare for all is one way to assure that rich and poor and everyone in between receives equally bad healthcare. Think about the result of the landmark legislation, the Affordable Care Act. It gave a lot more people access to a fundamentally broken, fragmented, expensive, inequitable and occasionally unsafe healthcare system...and hoped the system would heal itself. For all the reasons pointed out in our call to action, the system didn't change, partly because it didn't have to and because it was easier to keep the status quo. That can't happen again.

5

Policy for Health Assurance

U.S. healthcare policies have long tended to support and often enrich the incumbent healthcare industry—which means the policies were good for healthcare systems but not for consumers and not for innovative companies trying to better serve consumers. Many of those policies are now, in the wake of Covid, likely to change faster than anyone had anticipated.

How Ro saw this play out is one good example.

Zach Reitano has been very open about why he co-founded Ro. While in his twenties, he suffered from erectile dysfunction because of a heart condition. He was lucky—his father was a physician, so getting ED medication was not difficult. But his situation made Reitano aware that for most men, finding a physician to diagnose ED and prescribe medication can be arduous and embarrassing, and pills such as Viagra, Levitra and Cialis are often not covered by insurance and cost hundreds of dollars for just a few doses.

Reitano thought there had to be a way to use technology to help men with ED—a way that would put the consumer first. Ro's challenges as it tried to help its customers has implications for how we can scale care during a pandemic.

In October 2017, Reitano, Saman Rahmanian and Rob Schutz founded what was then called Roman. The site would let men talk to or email a doctor online, avoiding the hassle of going to a doctor's office and the difficulty of talking about the problem face-to-face. Then the company would set up a monthly subscription by mail, charging far less than pharmacies. (Mailing the pills also eliminated trips to the drugstore and the possibility of a clerk announcing to all the store patrons, "Mr. So-and-so, please pick up your Viagra.")

A service such as Ro's seems like an all-around good thing for consumers, allowing men with ED to get a life-enhancing, safe treatment in a way that's easier and cheaper than it had ever been. But healthcare regulations—most of them put in place decades ago—aren't set up to let that easily happen.

All 50 states issue their own medical licenses. That arrangement made some sense when doctors almost always practiced locally. (Though it's also been a way for physician groups to limit competition in their markets.) Going into the pandemic, it was a significant barrier to letting doctors practice virtually. A physician in Boston who only had a Massachusetts license couldn't get online with a patient in Bozeman, Montana, and prescribe medication. For Ro (the company changed its name once it got into products for women, too), the licensing restrictions meant that the company had to employ doctors in every state, or help doctors go through expensive, time-consuming licensing applications in multiple states—and do it every year, since licenses must be renewed annually. The process was so burdensome that in 2018 there were just 14 doctors licensed in all 50 states and the District of Columbia, according to the Federation of State Medical Boards.

Consider how different that is from banking and automatic teller machines. Until the early 1990s, regulators treated banking as a local industry, so banks faced obstacles to doing business outside of their home states. An ATM card from a bank in Virginia might not work in Texas—an enormous roadblock to convenient consumer banking in an era of increasing mobility and travel. In 1994, Congress passed the Riegle–Neal Interstate Banking and Branching Efficiency Act, which essentially permitted true nationwide banking—and ATM use—for the first time. ATMs became truly useful and thus became part of everyday life for most Americans.

The same thing must happen for virtual medicine.

To add to the barriers to Ro's style of virtual medicine, each state and D.C. has its own pharmacy license. In order to send pills anywhere in the U.S., Ro needs to maintain 51 pharmacy licenses. Add it up, and Ro must deal with 102 regulatory agencies plus federal agencies like the FDA. Of course, all of that added cost and time to everything Ro was doing. "I understand having a law that says a physician needs a license to practice, or a pharmacy needs a license to operate," Reitano says. "But the human body is the same in every state."

If the law would put consumers first, having one medical license that works in the whole country—like any state's driver's license—would make more sense. It would open the way not just for Ro, but for a flourishing of virtual medicine and other companies that take a consumer-driven approach to care. People in small rural towns would be able to consult with top doctors in major cities. Competition would be unleashed, lowering prices for physician services. The lower barriers to seeing a doctor might mean that more people consult a virtual doctor and catch problems earlier, avoiding more serious illnesses. Oh, and if doctors in offices spend less time seeing patients with minor problems that are easily dealt with online, they will have more time to spend with patients who need serious help in person.

The benefits of such a policy became clear during the Covid pandemic. As doctors and hospitals in hotspots were overwhelmed with Covid patients, they needed to direct people to first be evaluated online. As patients flocked to telehealth, those services connected patients in overwhelmed hotspot zones to medical professionals who were less busy in places where Covid hadn't yet hit as hard. In fact, that realization led the Trump administration to allow Medicare to pay for telehealth consultations for the first time. But that just shows how outmoded the old scheme is, and why it should be permanently changed before the next wave of Covid comes...or the next pandemic.

Across the board, healthcare policy has not caught up to today's digital, mobile and social era, and definitely is not set up for pandemics. Too often, policies protect a broken healthcare system. If we're ever to reinvent healthcare—if we're determined to create a new category of health assurance with consumers at the center—policy must be reinvented, too.

And that's an important opportunity. Entrepreneurs and innovators must be part of the change. They must understand policy and regulation, and help educate policymakers.

Societies want to keep their citizens safe from bad practices and dangerous substances. There must be a way to make sure every person has access to decent care—which now includes making sure every person has access to modern communication tools. There must be a way to make sure families don't go bankrupt because someone gets sick or old.

In the U.S., healthcare policy must evolve in a way that most politicians haven't so far been willing to consider. A sweeping policy like

"Medicare for all" is neither the answer nor is likely to be politically viable. The answer is more nuanced and must change as technology advances and the industry shifts to health assurance.

* * *

Healthcare policy and regulations are a daunting morass. The Affordable Care Act was 2,300 pages when it passed. By 2016, policymakers had added 16,000 pages of regulations. If we get into the weeds on healthcare policy here, we'll never hack our way out.

Most of the debate about healthcare policy has focused on how to help people pay for care that is too expensive. That is the wrong debate. What must change about policy are the overarching design principles. Policy should focus on how to allow the system to reinvent itself while keeping consumers safe and making sure everyone has access to basic care.

Entrepreneurs and innovators must become involved. Startups must form leadership teams that include experts in medicine and policy. Innovation in this field can't be "move fast, break things and apologize later." Medicine is not an industry that will be "disrupted" in a jiffy—but it is now more vulnerable to outside forces and more open to change than ever. Founders must leap on this opportunity to change the whole system by working closely with policymakers, regulators and healthcare professionals.

The goal is to migrate from the healthcare model of last century, which sidelined consumers, to health assurance, which puts consumers first. To get there, we propose 10 principles of health assurance policy design.

1. Reward health, not sickness.

The best healthcare policy would drive down the use of healthcare. To echo this book's opening, what we all really want is to stay as healthy as possible and spend as little time as possible in doctors' offices and hospitals. Over the next couple of years, as societies everywhere try to get past Covid, that will to be important. We should think of healthcare the way we now think of energy: we want to reward using less.

The old healthcare industry was set up to reward everyone in the system when people used healthcare more. Insurance has always paid a fee for service—for an office visit, a surgical cut, an X-ray, an IV drip. Insurers rarely pay for health. A physician who keeps her patients so healthy they never come in would make a lot less money than a terrible physician whose patients constantly get sick and need help. In the old system, more people made more money when more people were sick. (Though hospitals lost tens of millions of dollars when they were overrun during the worst of Covid with patients who couldn't pay while at the same time losing lucrative elective surgeries.)

Any policy that upholds that old status quo is counter-productive.

Over the past decade, policies have nudged the industry toward paying for quality and outcomes rather than fee-for-service. Most healthcare industry leaders know that's the right direction. But progress has been slow. And that has taken its toll on companies developing health assurance services intended to keep people healthy instead of just treating them once they're sick.

Mindstrong is an example. As its website says: "Our technology helps us predict how you're doing. We'll reach out if we think you might need support." A user downloads an app on his or her phone, and the software then watches how that person types, taps and uses apps. By analyzing such actions, the software can tell if cognitive function is declining—perhaps a precursor to the person becoming depressed or entering into a bout of PTSD—and recommend preemptive action that might keep that person out of a hospital. That is obviously a better strategy than, say, treating people after they've tried to hurt themselves. Yet the health system is not set up to pay for and reward such a service. If no medical action is taken, there's no billing code to send to the insurance company for reimbursement. Yet the system would pay for treating a severe PTSD attack that lands a patient in a hospital. That's wrong.

If we're to reinvent healthcare and bring to life health assurance, policies must curtail fee-for-service healthcare and favor practices, products and services that keep people healthy and out of the "sick care" system.

2. Create an environment conducive to open innovation.

The healthcare system has long thrown up enormous impediments to innovations that might reinvent care. Yes, technology has always brought near-miracles to medicine, whether it's the MRI, robots for precision surgery, or artificial body parts. But the way patients access and interact with the system hasn't changed much in 30 years.

We're inventing technologies that can transform the very model of healthcare—the way it's delivered, the way it's consumed, the way people work. Yet it's been too easy for the healthcare system to reject such change. The good news here is that Covid took a hammer to some of that resistance.

At Commure, the idea is to build a platform for healthcare apps, something like the app platforms for Apple's iOS or Google's Android. If you think about those platforms, developers can build an app once for anyone to use. Data can migrate between apps—your GPS location data, for instance, can move into the Uber app; an appointment set by email can automatically populate your calendar.

Nothing like that exists for healthcare apps. Data about patients or outcomes or anything else usually is locked up inside a healthcare system or a stand-alone electronic medical record system, blocked from being shared with other apps. If an app is developed for one healthcare system, it is often incompatible with the technology from other systems. Developers can't independently build an app that all systems can easily adopt. All of that is a drag on innovation, and it actually threatened lives during Covid, when physicians could not get data they needed about patients and governments couldn't get population data that might have helped with Covid-related decisions.

If policy is to aid innovation, it must prevent health systems from hoarding or blocking data. Policy must encourage the kind of openness we see in software elsewhere. It's already moving in the right direction. The 21st Century Cures Act, signed in 2016 by President Obama, includes provisions that push for greater interoperability of software and more open data. Lobbyists and entrenched interests still try to derail some of the provisions. Entrepreneurs and innovators must help policymakers and health professionals embrace open innovation and strengthen rules that support it.

3. Put consumers in charge of their data.

Data is the fuel that drives health assurance. Data about users is key to helping them stay healthy, predict problems and spend less money and time on "sick care."

Services like Livongo will collect and analyze more and more new kinds of health data about users. Livongo uses AI to get to know its users through data. Color, 23andMe and other genomics companies are collecting unprecedented amounts of data about people's DNA. All of that data must belong to users, and the federal rules released in March 2020 will help make that possible. Users must be able to decide what to do with their data, whether that means allowing an app to access it, sending it to a new doctor or allowing medical researchers to use it. Strong privacy laws must protect it.

Your records should be in the cloud and the doctors you use can have a password to see them. If you want to change your cardiologist, you just change that password to grant access and block the old cardiologist. There is no reason your data shouldn't be safely in your control.

Policymakers generally understand this imperative. In 2010, the U.S. Veterans Administration launched its "Blue Button" initiative—on the VA website, patients could click a blue button and download their medical records. The Centers for Medicare and Medicaid Services (CMS) started a Blue Button initiative later that year. A Blue Button 2.0 is an attempt to increase adoption of data and API standards. The latest HHS rules giving patients the right to their data further this trend.

As of early 2020, awareness and usage of the data downloads remained narrow. But at least it's a start. Policy must continue in that direction in order for health assurance to work.

4. Give patients the power to be informed consumers.

Patients still have little ability to make informed choices about their care. Health systems and insurance companies guard information about pricing and outcomes. If you need knee surgery, you have almost no way to compare prices and quality around the country and choose where to go. You can find far more information about a flight on a site like Expedia than you can about the doctor who's about to cut you open.

If today's healthcare is to transform into consumer-first health assurance, we will all need the power to act like consumers. That means prices must be transparent to all of us, and we must have access to data about the quality of care provided by doctors, clinics, hospitals and so on.

That doesn't mean just publishing price lists so we know that an Advil given in an emergency room costs $40. Policy should demand that patients can understand what to expect and what they will pay for it. If you are considering knee-replacement surgery and you like 10K runs, you want to know from each hospital: what you will pay out of pocket; the chance of you running that distance in six months; the hospital's complication rate, and what other patients have said about that hospital and surgeon. After all, it's what you'd expect when assessing contractors to renovate your kitchen.

Jefferson is developing a "match.com" type of service for obstetric patients and their providers that will be available on the Commure platform. It will bring to each consumer the power to determine the best healthcare professional to partner with for one of the most important events of her life based on real outcomes, patient comments and services provided—as opposed to a "referral" from a physician or an insurer.

5. Assure everyone access to good, affordable care, with premium services on top of that.

In the U.S.—in fact, in many developed countries—policy favors the concept that everyone should have equal access to all healthcare. (Canada, for instance, makes private healthcare illegal. All healthcare must be part of the national system.) A McDonald's burger flipper should be able to get the same high-tech heart surgery and hospital room as a hedge fund billionaire. While that sounds egalitarian and utopian, it's not ideal.

Everyone should be assured of access to good healthcare that allows them to thrive and avoid bankruptcy. They should be able to see a capable doctor when sick, have access to services that will help them stay healthy, receive the medication they are prescribed, and have access to the procedures they need.

And yet, if that's where it ends—if those who can afford premium services aren't allowed to pay for them—no one will develop expensive new treatments or expectation-breaking high-class hospital rooms that insurance won't cover. We as a society want entrepreneurs and innovators to develop advanced technology that may not be accessible to everyone. As we've seen with technology throughout history—TV, cell phones, genetic sequencing—a breakthrough invention that starts out as too expensive for the masses usually becomes cheaper as it scales. If we want to drive more innovation faster in health assurance, developers must be encouraged to create breakthrough, pricey products that can be made affordable to more people later. In fact, it's the responsibility of technologists in this sector to make sure this happens.

Think of it like the airline industry. The bulk of passengers are in coach. A handful of well-off people paid many times more for a ticket in first class. The experience is different, but all the passengers get to the destination safely and at the same time. Or consider telecommunications. In 1934, the U.S. passed a law ensuring "universal service"—every person who wanted a telephone landline must be able to get one. But that law didn't prevent companies from building premium services that were unaffordable to a large swath of the population. Such services, like long-distance calling and, later, cell phones, eventually became cheaper and more accessible.

Health policy should similarly assure good care for everyone, while making gold and even platinum service available for those who can afford it.

That's why we believe a plan like "Medicare for all" would ensure that everyone gets the same level of mostly-bad healthcare. On the other end of the political spectrum, too much deregulation would create an enormous divide: the rich would receive great care and stay healthy while those with lower incomes would find care inaccessible and become sick. Neither policy position seems like a good solution. We have learned the hard way that a virus crosses class lines—if we don't protect the poor from becoming sick, we'll all be sick.

The promise of health assurance is that it will drive down the cost of staying healthy. Health assurance for all will cost less than paying for "sick care" for all.

But that also means policymakers must make sure every individual has access to at least basic health assurance services. That might include giving everyone a free virtual health app that allows 24/7 access to an online doctor, either through a smartphone or at kiosks that could be set up on sidewalks, at pharmacies, in churches, in shelters or anywhere else. It might even include policies that go beyond healthcare and assure that every adult has a device with internet access—a policy that could have positive implications on other things like education and social services.

6. Focus on safety, less on efficacy.

In medicine, most new products and services—pills, devices, procedures—must receive regulatory approval before being offered to the public. That's a good thing. No one wants to go back to the days of snake-oil salesmen marketing a mixture of alcohol and molasses as a cure for gout.

Regulations demand that something new be both safe and effective. In other words, developers must prove their product or service won't harm most people (just about every drug has negative side-effects for some portion of the population) and will significantly help most people (though nothing works on everyone, every time). Those requirements make securing regulatory approval—and offering new stuff to the public—much more burdensome than it has should. It is an impediment to innovation in health assurance, and to reacting quickly with new services when something like Covid rolls in.

This tension between safety and efficacy can be seen in policies that have hampered Livongo's ability to innovate as much as it would like. The company went through traditional FDA approval processes, and showed regulators that its wireless glucometer, app and service met their safety threshold and helped users. The efficacy part took much longer because it was necessary to document user experiences over time. Eventually, the company won approval for what Livongo offered at that time.

But now thousands of users have digital wireless Livongo devices that could be upgraded, or packed with added software features and services. But Livongo can't easily do that because the company would have to go back to regulators to be approved for safety and then...with more user experience and more time...for efficacy. If the only proof point were safety, Livongo could more quickly roll features out to its users, and then track effectiveness or let users decide what to use or discard. The efficacy part delays getting potentially helpful features into users' hands.

Think of your smartphone and how often the software is updated and features are added, and how many apps you've downloaded—some of which you've come to love and some of which you've deleted. That allows innovation to happen quickly.

We would never advocate that regulators let up on safety. But in this era of Google, social media and data, proving efficacy before going to market seems less important. We'll all know soon if something works—especially once we move further into health assurance and much of the population has real-time data and digital medical records that researchers could study (anonymized, of course).

We need regulators to think of digital health assurance products the same way they would think about any other technology. Make sure a product is safe. Let consumers decide how good it is.

7. Don't protect the status quo, and help health assurance emerge.

Health assurance is not meant to displace the legacy healthcare system—a $4 trillion industry in America. We're not proposing destruction of what exists. The only way health assurance will happen is if the current U.S. healthcare ecosystem plays a role in building it.

Policymakers who embrace the development of health assurance must realize that the legacy healthcare industry needs help to move in that direction. Any policy that helps the current industry resist change will slow developments that will bring consumers a better care experience. The shift to health assurance is inevitable.

The best policies will help current healthcare players disrupt themselves and endure.

For example, well meaning twentieth-century policy subsidizes hospitals that lose business, with the intention of keeping hospitals open in more communities. But that rewards costly physical hospitals when hospital systems must migrate to "hospitals with no address"—virtualized hospitals that might start with an online doctor visit and end with a patient directed to a nearby clinic or a specialized surgical center. Society doesn't need more scaled-up hospitals that would be half-empty most of the time just to be ready for the next pandemic. We need a flexible, resilient health system that can use software, cloud computing and AI to treat more people virtually, let more patients recover at home, and quickly redeploy precious hardware and professionals to where they are most needed. It sounds counter-intuitive, but Covid taught us that we actually need fewer hospital beds and more flexible, virtual healthcare.

Similarly, policy should not protect insurance companies from losing their highly profitable role as middlemen. It should help them migrate to acting as valuable data suppliers or, perhaps, aggregators of health assurance services. Policy shouldn't protect the profits of pharmaceutical companies, but instead help them become consumer-facing companies that compete transparently on price and value.

Importantly, policy should fan the embers of health assurance. During Covid, some insurance companies and Medicare began paying for telehealth and virtual visits, and such services exploded. Those changes should be cemented in place and built upon.

Protecting the legacy healthcare industry would be like trying to protect the movie industry from VCRs in the 1980s. The movie industry thought that allowing people to record or play movies at home would destroy its business model. It lobbied forcefully for protection. Its leaders couldn't see that by participating in the movies-at-home revolution instead of fighting against it, profitability would explode. We are at a similar inflection point for the current healthcare industry. Policy that pushes the healthcare industry to participate in health assurance can be a boon for the incumbents who join the transformation.

8. Reposition and retrain healthcare professionals and workers.

The U.S. healthcare industry employs nearly 20 million people. They became our heroes during the Covid crisis, and we must treat them as such as the industry shifts. The truth that almost all of them will see their jobs change dramatically or be eliminated in the next 10 years. Policy must address this, or the disruption will be devastating to families and the economy.

Artificial intelligence and other technologies are about to vastly alter the role of a doctor. Society—from medical schools to licensing regimes to professional organizations—must help transform how we select and educate physicians. Doctors in the era of health assurance will need to score high in empathy, communication and creativity—subjects not at the core of most med school programs. The best doctors will also know how to take advantage of the analytical power of AI.

The rest of the workforce will need a huge retraining effort because the hospital will no longer serve as the center of the healthcare ecosystem. Training for telehealth workers, providers who go to patients' homes, genetic counselors, predictive risk managers, customer experience professionals and population health professionals will be imperative.

AI-driven software bots will in many cases become the initial interaction for a patient, freeing up the doctor, nurse, pharmacist or other healthcare professional to spend more time with patients who need the human touch. Consumers will get the best of both worlds—a gentle hand and the aid of augmented intelligence.

Policymakers who believe this transition will be bad for healthcare professionals haven't been paying attention. A 2019 survey by the National Academy of Medicine, one of the country's most prestigious medical institutions, found that nearly half of U.S. doctors and nurses suffer from extreme burnout. That leads to emotional exhaustion, cynicism, loss of enthusiasm and joy in their work, and increasing detachment from their patients and their patients' ailments. Worse, the burnout is linked to higher rates of depression, substance abuse and suicide. The suicide rate among physicians is one of the highest among all professions. The report put the blame squarely on a dysfunctional U.S. healthcare system, primarily because physicians are doing less of what they went into healthcare to do: help patients who need human interaction. A transformed health assurance model will alleviate many of the burdensome administrative and technological roadblocks that prevent doctors and nurses from doing what they do best.

9. Get ahead of AI.

Artificial intelligence has enormous potential to change health and medicine. It is the key to building technology that allows professionals to deliver empathy at scale. Yet like any powerful new technology, AI comes with a potential to do harm. Good policy will get out in front of that possible harm, not react to it after it's too late.

Companies typically use AI algorithms to optimize their businesses. Uber efficiently dispatches its drivers during rush hour, Facebook displays the most relevant stories to its users and Amazon can suggest the right product at the optimal time to drive a purchase. For all their positives, what algorithms aren't optimized for is doing the *right* thing or for displaying any transparency. From the outside, there's no understanding of how decisions are made inside those software-driven black boxes, and no way to know if the companies are overtly or inadvertently behaving badly. The algorithms that manage internal operations strongly favor doing whatever is the most expedient, efficient and effective, even if that means, for instance, amplifying societal biases.

The last thing anyone wants is for health assurance AI to treat people differently because of the way they look, or their income, or where they live. Or for health AI to put patients at risk for the sake of profits.

Another concern with AI: it's only as good as the data that feeds it. Most health data today is oriented toward billing and procedures, not toward information pertinent to an individual's health. Regulators must pay attention not just to algorithms, but to what kinds of data are going into those algorithms.

AI technology is developing so quickly, we're concerned that the usual processes for making policy or regulations will be too slow. One solution would be to adopt software-defined regulation, which can monitor software-driven industries better than regulations enforced by squads of regulation bureaucrats.

Algorithms can "watch" emerging services, seeing details and patterns that humans might never catch. Consider Uber. If transportation officials who regulated taxis want to make sure Uber doesn't shun certain neighborhoods or bias its service, they should write an algorithm to look for the behavior and automatically take action if necessary.

Such watchdog algorithms can be like open-source software—open to examination by anyone. That way, coders can see if the watchdog algorithms are monitoring the right things, while the companies keep private proprietary algorithms and data. How to create software-defined regulation? Regulators define the rules, technologists create the software to implement them and then AI can help refine iterations of policies going forward.

While that may seem like an outside-the-box concept, it's worth pursuing rather than risk the alternative. A lack of AI policy in healthcare would be disastrous. But so would bad policy that results in stagnant regulations that could stifle an emerging industry.

In the meantime, we encourage the health assurance industry to be intensely mindful of building ethical AI, or risk a public and regulatory backlash. AI can do its job only if it's trusted. Loss of trust could derail health assurance.

10. Stop trying to pass a "Big Bang" solution.

Finally, even during this post-Covid strategic inflection point for healthcare, we believe that policy change should be constantly evolving, not the kind of major, all-encompassing legislation that often is proposed. The only certainty is that things will continue to change, often in ways no one can foresee. The technology that drives health assurance is still evolving. As the technology improves, new business models and new kinds of services will be imagined and implemented. That in turn will create jobs that don't yet exist—and problems we can't foresee.

The best policies will put up guardrails that help make sure health assurance emerges the way we want it to and keeps the public safe, while allowing entrepreneurs and innovators to move the industry forward and leave the old, dysfunctional system behind.

6

Company Design for Health Assurance

Now more than ever, the world needs new kinds of companies that blend a Silicon Valley, software-driven, change-the-world mentality with the experience, empathy and vision of healthcare leaders. These blended skills will move us from a broken "sick care" system to the new category of innovation called health assurance.

Health assurance companies bring modern consumer experiences to healthcare with a real commitment to decreasing the healthcare GDP as a whole. Health assurance companies accelerate rational economic behavior with innovative business models and price transparency in their offerings. Health assurance companies are built on principles of open technology standards, empathetic user design and responsible AI to empower the healthcare workforce and put consumers in control of their own health.

We know this category and we know that partnerships between tech and healthcare can work because we—Hemant and Steve—are living it. This is the story of Commure, a company Hemant co-founded to make health assurance a reality.

This story starts in 2016. Hemant, who'd helped build Livongo, saw that it was growing as fast as any software company in Silicon Valley. He started to think about the next health assurance company he could start with his firm, General Catalyst—one that could help other health assurance companies bloom. General Catalyst looks to hatch new businesses with great co-founders, and it so happened that a few months later, Hemant went on a trip to India with Diede van Lamoen, who was building out the international business for payments platform Stripe (another company funded by General Catalyst). Van Lamoen's challenge was to get Stripe's platform running in the different regulatory environments of multiple countries. He and Hemant joked that it was probably easier to launch a payments platform in another country than bring innovation to a U.S. hospital.

On the trip, they talked about healthcare and about electronic medical records that were set up to maximize billing, which means they don't tell a doctor what she needs to know about a patient's health and lifestyle. Plus, electronic records and data are stored in applications that can't talk to each other, making it difficult to layer data to get a complete picture of a patient. Worst of all, the technology requires doctors to enter information, which means they are paying attention to computer screens while seeing a patient...instead of paying attention to the patient. Hemant and van Lamoen decided to be serious about building a solution to this fundamental issue.

Back in the U.S., the two visited hospitals to see how doctors worked, and sought advice from experts such as Bill Brody, the former president of Johns Hopkins University, and Bob Wachter, chairman of the University of California, San Francisco, Department of Medicine and author of *The Digital Doctor*. The chief technology officer of Dropbox, Quentin Clark, also began to help architect the cloud framework for the platform. Eugene Kuznetsov, a co-founder of

Datapower, joined the team as a co-founder. A company was coming together, and the timing seemed right. The industry was feeling the pain of antiquated software; burnout was becoming a crisis; cloud computing companies were eyeing the industry; FHIR was emerging as a standard that allows data to be more easily shared; and legislation and regulations were slowly opening the industry to innovation. Tech entrepreneurs all over the country were starting to pay attention.

But the company needed healthcare partners to gain traction. In the spring of 2018, Hemant and Kuznetsov hosted a dinner at a Las Vegas healthcare conference and invited senior leaders from the industry to talk about innovation and change. Among those invited was Steve. During the dinner, Steve pointed out that he and many other CEOs were caught in the paradox of simultaneously scaling to survive in the short term so they'd be able to unscale later, creating what he called "healthcare with no address"—virtual healthcare that doesn't rely on treating sick people in big hospitals, instead bringing affordable and desirable care to consumers where they needed it. Steve said just needed technology that could help him do that, and no such technology existed.

Hemant knew technologists had largely failed to build successful health applications on their own. Healthcare is not a free market, where developers can just barge in and reinvent things. On the other hand, insiders rarely had the outside-the-box thinking or chutzpah to use technology to radically change their industry. The only path forward was a partnership. That's why Hemant asked Steve to join the effort to build Commure.

As an all-in partner, Steve brought much-needed firepower. At the same time, the leadership of Boston Children's Hospital, which had helped develop the FHIR standard, signed on to partner with the company.

So what is Commure? (The name combines the words "community" and "care.") It's a platform that can host healthcare applications and connect their data. By pulling in traditional data from health records, X-rays, lab tests and such, and adding new kinds of data generated by consumer-facing applications like Livongo or Mindstrong or a fitness or sleep tracker, Commure makes it possible for a physician or any other care-team member to see a more complete view of a patient. All of that data can be run through an artificial intelligence that learns about a patient, perhaps spotting stroke symptoms or those of another event, and offers proactive suggestions to help the patient avoid that trauma.

By helping data flow in a more automated way, such a system can free doctors from data entry, allowing them instead time to be empathetic, highly-skilled physicians. In that way, technology can help bring more humanity to medicine.

We intentionally built Commure in a new way, learning from mistakes and breakthroughs. Every health tech company now must think this way. Our goal is to see thousands of startups like Livongo, Ro, Color and Mindstrong bloom and enable the health assurance industry, and we wholeheartedly believe that we'll eventually see a dozen or more new multi-billion-dollar companies in this space.

So, with that in mind, the rest of this chapter is about how to design a health assurance company and some of the opportunities we see in this emerging category.

* * *

Regardless of your innovation or the market space you're pursuing in health assurance, we believe that a set of design principles will be key to creating an impactful and responsible company. Here are those principles:

Above all, build with empathy.

Merriam-Webster defines empathy as: "the action of understanding, being aware of, being sensitive to, and vicariously experiencing the feelings, thoughts, and experience of another of either the past or present without having the feelings, thoughts, and experience fully communicated in an objectively explicit manner." Oddly and sadly, this is something both the tech and healthcare industries have lost.

Technologists in the 2010s tended to be more concerned with building cool stuff, finding something to "disrupt," and making money. This is how we ended up with the caustic early years of Uber, the uncivil attitude of Facebook and the hubris of WeWork. Meanwhile, the healthcare industry is filled with people who got into the field because they wanted to help people, and then found that the industry over-values efficiency, procedure and, like tech, making money. The business can suck the passion and idealism out of young physicians.

This must stop. The only technology that will truly reinvent healthcare is technology that prioritizes empathy. Electronic medical records systems are designed to increase efficiency and billing, not foster empathy in the doctor–patient relationship. A watch or wearable that tracks your vital signs may be a cool bit of engineering, but it doesn't know who you are or understand your needs.

The wonder of artificial intelligence is that it can understand individuals at scale, so it can replicate some of the touch of an old-school family doctor at a cost that makes it affordable to bring that kind of care to everyone. We founded Livongo on that principle—we wanted to build technology that could understand every individual's unique diabetic condition, and help them manage it in a way that fits into their lifestyles. And we founded Commure with the idea that AI can help medical professionals access deep information about their patients while taking away mundane record-keeping tasks, so doctors can spend more time listening to patients and being human.

If you are an entrepreneur or innovator, build to create empathy, not kill it. Think through how your product will make the user feel cared for, or how it will help a healthcare professional be more caring and communicative. Be empathetic: vicariously experience the feelings of the consumers and patients you will ultimately impact.

Partner, don't disrupt.

At the end of the 2010s, Silicon Valley was getting the message that its culture of "move fast and break things" was increasingly unwelcome. Technology "broke" some things that were quite valuable, like retail stores and journalism, without thinking through the consequences. Breaking healthcare would be an even more dangerous proposition.

Haven is an example of what not to do. Haven is a joint venture created by Amazon, Berkshire Hathaway and JPMorgan Chase. It's intended to improve healthcare while lowering costs for the combined companies' two million workers and their family members, relying heavily on technology to get there. The outcome may prove good for those three companies, but it will likely make healthcare worse for everyone else by taking insured (and thus profitable) patients out of the market and leaving healthcare systems to care for a higher percentage of the uninsured, which will eat up resources and chip away at quality.

New technologies should aim to make the industry better rather than work against it. Tech and healthcare must work together to reinvent a system everyone agrees is broken, ending the dominance of fee-for-service "sick care" and replacing it with a health assurance industry oriented toward keeping people healthy and out of hospitals and doctors' offices.

Assembling the right team is mission-critical. If you're a founder and look around the room and see a leadership team packed with technologists and MBAs, with maybe a physician on the board, you're in trouble. Similarly, if healthcare executives hire some coders and instruct them to build technology to make something more efficient, that's not going to work. Successful health assurance companies will have leadership teams balanced between tech and healthcare—with a health policy expert in the mix, too.

Redefine what market leadership means in this segment.

It's become doctrine in Silicon Valley that digital markets are always winner-take-all. That's how we got one dominant search company, one dominant social network, one dominant online retailer, and so on. Founders tend to race to get a minimal viable product to market, race to scale, race to hire, race to raise enormous rounds of funding—a race to be the winner. But that race can lead to management mistakes, products that hurt people, and toxic workplace cultures.

In healthcare, we believe a winner-take-all mentality is both unnecessary and dangerous.

Why unnecessary? Americans will spend around $4 trillion on healthcare in 2020. No single winner will take all of that. If you break healthcare down into smaller segments, they're all still enormous. Take diabetes, Livongo's market. The American Diabetes Association says that in 2018, spending on diabetes in the U.S. hit $327 billion. How can there not be room for multiple winners and approaches in a segment that size? How about mental health? The U.S. government estimates that we'll spend $238 billion on it in 2020. Lots of room for many approaches to reinventing mental health care.

And why is a winner-take-all mentality dangerous? That should be obvious. Unlike with search or social networks or retail, lives are at stake here. Medical products that do harm have disastrous consequences for individuals. In fact, bad products would have disastrous consequences for the whole health assurance movement. It wouldn't take many tragedies to turn the healthcare industry, general public and policymakers against technology and innovation.

Do not rush to beat or growth-hack around competition. Build with intentionality and responsibility.

Don't prioritize efficiency.

Health assurance is not about making the sick care system more efficient. It's about reinventing healthcare and keeping people as healthy as possible so they don't need sick care.

That means making products that are effective, not efficient. Focus on solving simple problems first, then earn the right to tackle bigger problems. Help people live healthier so you earn their trust and earn their data. Use that data to evolve into an AI company that people trust.

Never rush this process. If you can't help people, no amount of efficiency will save you. We can't state this too strongly: *build responsibly*.

Think market-segment personas.

Healthcare is not a giant monolith to attack. Countless segments have very specific needs, and all could benefit from a specialized approach to health assurance. Smart founders must understand that geriatric patients have different needs than pediatric patients; a 50-year-old man with erectile dysfunction has different concerns than a 50-year-old woman entering menopause.

Smart health assurance founders will think about segmentation in new ways. The medical field has long funneled all patients through primary care, as if the same kind of physician should be the healthcare quarterback no matter what's going on with a person's health. But care should be organized around a person's dominant condition. New kinds of primary care should address different segments: people with diabetes, women who are pregnant, seniors with dementia. Such thinking about market segments should also engender ideas for better serving markets that have difficulty accessing healthcare, such as people with lower incomes. We earlier described Sesame, which found a market niche in offering coupon-like discounts for things like MRI scans and physical therapy.

Build health assurance services that always put the individual first and act as that specific person's quarterback, simplifying and streamlining care in ways the current system can't.

Measure success by disengagement.

The point of health assurance is to minimize healthcare. No one wants to constantly think about his or her illness, or about how to stay healthy. Technologists too often measure success by clicks or eyeballs or time spent on a site. Throw those metrics away in health assurance.

The most effective products in health assurance will be the ones that make people almost forget they're using them. Innovation must remove the patient burden as much as possible.

The same can be said for innovations aimed at healthcare professionals. The sin of electronic health record technologies of the 2010s is that it required more and more attention from doctors and nurses, taking them away from patients. Think about this: More and more health systems are hiring scribes so the doctor–patient relationship can be maintained. No doctor should be entering information on a screen while in a room with a patient. Successful health assurance technology will free doctors from paying attention to it.

Align incentives for payers, beneficiaries and decision-makers.

A big part of why the U.S. healthcare system is broken is that who pays (usually insurance companies) is separated from who benefits (the patient) and who decides on care (doctors). We doubt this can be fixed by technology or entrepreneurship alone. It will need an assist from smart policy.

And yet, we encourage entrepreneurs and innovators to think through how they might better align motivations. A subscription primary care company like Forward gets part-way there. A subscription model is typically paid for by the consumer, not the insurance company, which means the consumer decides on the best service at the price they want to pay. A subscription model also helps align the provider with the interests of consumers who want to stay as healthy as possible. The company isn't being paid per action, like in the fee-for-service model. In fact, the company makes more money when customers use its services less—and the best way for the company to keep you out of its facilities is to keep you as healthy as possible.

As more companies prove such an aligned model works, more consumers will want to shift to health assurance, and more policymakers will consider changes that allow health assurance to flourish.

Solve for resiliency.

In April 2020, as New York City lit up as the world's Covid hotspot and its hospitals seemed unprepared for the coming surge of patients, New York Governor Andrew Cuomo got on TV and talked about how the state and the nation needed to be able to move resources from hotspot to hotspot as the virus progressed. New York needed a flood of medical professionals, ventilators and other equipment now. In a few weeks, if pressure eased on New York hospitals but was ramping up in Chicago or Dallas, the staff and equipment should move there.

It's a shame that the governor had to propose a kind of responsive resource-sharing that never existed in healthcare at scale. Traditional healthcare has not been a resilient, flexible system, but now it must be. It's possible if we do more with software, do more to treat people at home, and overcome barriers that prevent care across state or national borders. Companies that step in and find ways to build such resilient care will play a crucial role in the next era of medicine.

* * *

Let's say you're an ambitious person and you've read this far and you're considering what kind of company or product to build. The possibilities are almost limitless. It's difficult to foresee the kaleidoscope of products that will be built because one breakthrough product will create layers of new possibilities, much as the iPhone opened up a world of apps like Uber or Shazam that no one, pre-iPhone, could've imagined.

That said, we can see some of what will be needed for health assurance. Here are some of the ways to think about companies and products in this space.

Targeted Markets

Consumer product companies do a great job of identifying personas and building products specifically for that group. Car companies make minivans for soccer moms and mini cars for urban dwellers. Clothing retailers develop a Victoria's Secret for women who want to look sexy and Hot Topic for teens who want to look like goth rockers.

Health assurance needs that kind of targeting, too—services for young mothers and services for grandmothers; for people in rural towns far from doctors; for people with every kind of chronic condition; for people trying to beat addiction; for athletes trying for peak performance; and on and on. Some of this segmentation has begun, and we will see winners in each category.

Understand who you're building for, then focus on empathy and health, not on treatment. The most successful products will be those that help your particular population forget about their health circumstances and stay healthy.

Analytics Platforms

Health assurance is all about data. As more apps and platforms are built, we'll have enormous flows of data, which medical professionals, providers and researchers will use to achieve new insights into health, consumer markets, and the way we live our lives. Analyzing this data will yield breakthroughs we can barely imagine, and will help physicians understand each patient in a holistic way.

But to get there, technology must bring together data and analyze it. Much of that field remains wide open.

"Back Office" Technology

Hemant was an early investor in Stripe. He saw the need for a company that could automate payments and other financial functions, taking that burden off of a startup company. Health assurance will need more of those kinds of services, built specifically for the sector. If we continue to spend $4 trillion a year on health, that's a lot of transactions to process.

We foresee the need for a payments company, and for similar companies that can automate compliance and governance in a highly-regulated sector.

"Cash Pay" Companies

Health assurance will increasingly decouple care from health insurance. As people abandon insurance, or don't have it because they or the business they work for can't afford it, we see a whole sector emerging for the cash-pay economy—people paying out of their own pockets.

The companies in this space won't look much like traditional healthcare companies. They will look more like consumer retailers. Prices will be transparent and sensible. Services will be rated and reviewed. Customers will be offered sales and specials—unheard of in traditional healthcare. If you want to see a forerunner of a cash pay health assurance company, take a look at Sesame, which offers discounts on medical care the way a grocery store might offer coupons for cereal.

Self-Insured Management

As health assurance replaces the misaligned economics of health insurance, increasing numbers of companies and institutions will self-insure—i.e., will directly pay for employee care. But to manage that, these companies will need technology services that don't exist.

Those services will help employers manage the enormous cost and complexity of self-insurance. They'll track spending and tie it to outcomes, helping companies understand which services work best for their population and which ones don't.

Companies don't want to be in the health assurance business—they want to tend to their business. New services that can take away that distraction will be crucial.

Healthcare Communication

If we're to reinvent care to consider the whole patient, a spectrum of health professionals—doctors, nurses, social workers, pharmacists, psychologists, personal trainers—will need to communicate and coordinate with each other and share information in ways that are highly reliable and ensure patient privacy.

One thing we can see: there will be a great need for some health assurance version of Slack, with each chat-room channel organized around a single patient, bringing together all the people who must talk to each other in order to treat a condition or keep that patient healthy. Perhaps we will need several Slacks, each built for a different market sector of health assurance.

AI-Assisted Care

Artificial intelligence will play a huge role in health assurance. More and better data will train AIs to learn more about individual patients and broadly about medical conditions.

As IBM's Watson has already shown at Cleveland Clinic and other healthcare facilities, AI can help physicians with diagnoses by acting as a kind of research assistant. Thousands of pages of medical research papers are produced every year, new drugs constantly enter the market, new procedures are perfected—there is no way any human doctor can keep up with all of that. But an AI can ingest all that information, listen to a doctor–patient conversation, and suggest questions and answers that will help a physician arrive at the right diagnosis.

AI will show up everywhere. AI-driven chat bots will "talk" to mental health patients—we already know that many younger people are more likely to be honest with a chat bot than a psychologist. AI will help keep an eye on seniors 24/7, enabling them to live at home longer. There will be opportunities for AI-driven care in every nook and cranny of health assurance.

Workforce Realignment

Many of the opportunities we just outlined—software-driven back office, self-insured management, AI-assisted care—will contribute to the elimination of many current back-office jobs. But that, too, is an opportunity. Society needs these skilled professionals. They must not be cast off, but instead be retrained for new roles in health assurance. Many could immediately be redeployed to telehealth or virtual home care. An entire industry can be built around that alone, and that would help care become more resilient and flexible.

7

Health Assurance and the Next Pandemic

Before the Covid-19 pandemic, health assurance was ramping up and pointing the way to a new era of care. Companies such as Livongo, Nuvo, Ro, Kinsa and others were proving that the approach, the technology and the business model all worked and created a good experience for users. At the same time, the old healthcare system was increasingly being seen as outdated, expensive and a bad consumer experience. The situation became ripe for health assurance to ascend and displace parts of the old system.

Covid stomped on the accelerator. It became healthcare's iPhone moment: all the conditions for creating a new concept were in place, and Covid became a catalyst that fused them and drove the concept into the mainstream.

The old system revealed itself to be inadequate to meet the crisis and nearly fell apart. Lives were saved because of the heroic efforts of doctors, nurses and other front-line workers—despite the shortcomings of the systems in which they worked.

Covid also showed why health assurance must be developed and deployed as quickly as possible. It will become critical to helping society navigate the coming year or two, as we all try to restore some semblance of normal life while managing the coronavirus that causes Covid-19. And health assurance technologies will play a crucial role in identifying and containing coming pandemics, which experts say will arrive more frequently.

If we put all the pieces together, this is a look at how health assurance will likely play out, and how it will help during pandemics.

As with any successful revolution, the transformation of healthcare will require multiple stakeholders deciding that they can no longer tolerate the current system. All of us must help to change a broken healthcare system into a better experience. Developers, entrepreneurs, healthcare professionals, policymakers, business leaders, patients and consumers all have roles to play.

In the next year or two, we believe one big change will be the rejection of what we now think of as health insurance, the layer between patient and provider. Covid will begin to stir a rebellion as millions of unemployed are faced with the cost of buying their own insurance, or going without and risking devastating medical bills—all while health insurers use Covid as a reason to hike premiums. More and more Americans were already finding that health insurance is a money pit. You pay a lot and still have a high deductible and copays, so insurance seems to do nothing for you unless you are seriously ill or injured. Meanwhile, insurance separates consumers from decisions about what to buy and how much to spend, which allows the whole healthcare system operate outside of normal economics. As health assurance begins to offer alternatives, the idea that an insurer pays for non-critical medical care will come to seem as outmoded as relying on a company pension as your sole resource for retirement.

Instead, we may see more people rely on a health assurance account, perhaps funded by employers (or by the government, instead of Medicare or Medicaid). We'll use such an account to pay for services that keep us healthy, such as routine doctor visits, health tech services, fitness training, and psychologists. Because each of us will be controlling the money, we'll make better decisions based on price and quality, which in turn will push the health assurance industry to be more competitive (unlike traditional healthcare).

For big health problems, many consumers will buy catastrophic insurance with a high deductible. It will work much like existing health insurance, but it will exist primarily to keep people from bankruptcy caused by serious health issues.

If you are generally healthy, you can use your health account to stay healthy. You will recognize that health is holistic, tying together your physical and mental state, what you eat, how you exercise, how you sleep, where you live, your income, your lifestyle and your genetics. You'll be able to use apps that tie all of that together and collect data from devices you wear or software you use. The data will feed an AI that can learn your patterns, nudge you toward better health, and watch for problems. The AI will know, for instance, that you are in danger of a heart attack—or may have caught a dangerous virus—long before you feel it. That will allow you to seek treatment before the condition becomes dangerous, and costly.

Whatever your most pressing health condition, you will find medical care that puts it at the center and builds all of your care around it. People with diabetes will find care oriented around that condition. The same will be true for someone who struggles with depression, women seeking to have children, or older people with dementia. Care will segment into narrow markets, much like many consumer products.

Sometimes, unfortunately, you'll be hurt or become seriously ill. Of course, that brings to mind what many have gone through during the Covid crisis. Before seeing a doctor, you'll talk to one on a video call. Many times, you'll get instructions on how to take care of the problem without going to the doctor's office. If you must go in, your visit will be a better experience than we usually have today. You'll make an appointment online and receive text updates if the doctor is running late. Waiting rooms will disappear. By the time you're in an examining room, the doctor will have already reviewed all your health data and will be able to focus on listening to you and then deducing what's wrong. A computer with AI will be listening, surfacing clues and information the doctor may not know, perhaps from recent studies or news the doctor would not have had time to read.

If you need drugs, the doctor plus AI will comb through your genomics subtypes and other data to identify drugs that will work best for you with the fewest side effects. No more trial and error. You'll always know exactly what a drug will cost and shop for the best way to get it, which will likely be through an online service that will deliver. No more waiting in pharmacy lines.

What's the catch? You, the consumer, must take more responsibility. Some might see that as a curse; others, as a blessing. You'll have more control over how your money is spent and make more decisions about products and services you buy based on information that's never been available before. You'll have to shift from thinking of healthcare as something someone else pays for, and and begin to think of it as something you pay for. But in return, you won't have to wrangle with insurance companies over what's covered, you'll know what you're getting at what price, the industry will compete harder for your business, you'll enjoy a much better experience, and ultimately you will spend less.

All of that describes health assurance for everyday life. At least for the near future, everyday life will include dodging or managing the coronavirus that causes Covid-19. Society knows the terrible cost of pandemics, and is ready to invest in ways to identify and contain the next one. Health assurance will play a significant role.

Let's assume that much of what we just described is being used by millions of people, and let's look at what a health assurance approach can do for us during a pandemic—and while we're waiting for the next one.

Start with yourself. If you're using health assurance services, then most of your health data is continuously streamed to the cloud. You can choose to have it flow into an AI-driven service that constantly analyzes data for patterns that indicate early symptoms of the new virus. The AI might also draw—in a privacy-protected manner—from your calendar or smartphone to see whether you've met with someone who also shows signs of the virus, or were in a location where others were infected. If it all adds up to a high probability that you have the virus, you'd be alerted so you can isolate yourself and avoid infecting family, friends and others around you.

You would then alert your physician through a telehealth app. The physician could see all your data, ask some questions, and become your coach throughout the course of the disease. You'd be sure to wear devices that would monitor your condition from home, including a pulse oximeter to measure oxygen in your blood and gadgets to track breathing, heart rate and temperature, all of them streaming data to the AI. The AI would continuously watch for alarming patterns. If the AI software senses a problem, it can alert you, a family member, and your physician, who can "see" you through the app.

All of this can be particularly important to people who live in rural areas. In many parts of the country, the nearest hospital is more than a 30-minute drive away and the nearest specialist may be a lot farther away than that. In this way, health assurance can bring good care to people who have access to almost no care now.[27]

In most cases, remote care will be enough. You will ride out the disease at home, yet have the comfort of knowing you are constantly monitored much as you would be in a hospital. (Actually, better.) This much, by itself, accomplishes a lot of good. It saves you the difficulty and cost of going to a doctor's office or emergency room. By giving you an early warning, it saves others around you from being infected, slowing the progression of the virus. The software monitoring and virtual visit saves your doctor time, so he or she can focus on listening to you and coaching you, and can do so for more patients than would be otherwise possible. The virtual nature of your care also means that local resources are not likely to be overwhelmed, so if your condition turns serious, you can get the hands-on care you need.

If you must go to the hospital, your data will arrive before you do. The doctor who sees you will know exactly what to do, without a second of wasted time. Because the hospital knows what to expect, staff can don the right equipment to protect themselves, which will help keep critical professionals healthy so they can treat more patients—and, of course, not endanger their own health. Once you're hooked up to hospital equipment, that data also goes to your AI and into your record, and that will help you and your doctor better manage your recovery after you leave the hospital.

Your data can also be anonymized, and flow to governments and researchers. (Technologists must develop strategies to convince us that we can trust sharing data while preserving our privacy.) Government

---

[27] "Where Americans Live Far From the Emergency Room," by Ella Koeze, Jugal K. Patel and Anjali Singhvi, *The New York Times*, April 26, 2020. https://www.nytimes.com/interactive/2020/04/26/us/us-hospital-access-coronavirus.html

officials will be able to track the virus in real-time. As they relax restrictions on movement or business, they can watch for signs of the virus re-emerging and make better decisions about how to contain it. The data might flow into a virus-tracking map that's available to the public, so people can make decisions about whether to go to a city that has a growing number of cases. The same data would help a business make plans to reopen an office in a region where the virus is trending down. All in all, the aggregation of health assurance data can help just about everyone better manage life during a pandemic, much as weather data and maps help officials and people manage life during hurricane season. In parallel, the data could be a help to researchers trying to understand the virus' behavior and develop treatments for Covid-19 and vaccinations to ward off the virus.

Once we get through this pandemic, most experts agree that it won't be long before another dangerous virus emerges. Aggregated, global health assurance data can play a game-changing role in identifying the next outbreak early, and keeping it from spreading and causing widespread damage. Once health assurance services are being used by millions of people all over the world, spikes in illnesses that indicate a viral outbreak could quickly be recognized. That region could be sealed off and individuals who show signs of having the virus, as seen by the data, would be told to quarantine. A global alert could let everyone know to be vigilant if they'd been in that region, and know to isolate if their data shows any sign of the contagion. Such early intervention may be enough to keep future novel viruses from spiraling into a pandemic.

We're likely only touching on the ways so much rich health data could help fight the next virus. Clever data scientists and medical researchers will no doubt use the data to better understand viruses, population health, human behavior and the effectiveness of government actions like business shutdowns, school closings and social distancing.

Health assurance is a path to a better, more equitable, more cost-effective healthcare experience for all consumers. It's a path to a better professional life for doctors, nurses and other healthcare professionals. And it can be an important component in keeping everyone safe from invisible enemies.

Now we have to build it, and here's what you can do:

Developers and Entrepreneurs

- Pick a segment or persona you have empathy for, and build products and services for that group.

- Partner with healthcare companies instead of seeing them as an old guard to be disrupted. Recognize that the new currency will be creative partnerships. The traditional healthcare ecosystem will have fewer dollars to spend on untested technology and more willingness to partner in revenue-sharing opportunities.

- Embed your engineers and developers deep inside healthcare provider systems so that you really know what patients and providers need as opposed to what you "think" they need.

- Build technology that generates new kinds of data, earn the trust of consumers, and use the data to train AI to serve customers in ever smarter and more targeted ways.

- Build responsibly, and understand that healthcare will always be heavily regulated. Work with policymakers to open the way for innovation while protecting consumers.

- Scale an ecosystem. Every market category will be big enough for many winners.

Healthcare Professionals, Executives and Innovators

- Embrace the concept of health assurance as a departure from the current fee-for-service model. Understand that there's more value in keeping people healthy and out of doctors' offices and hospitals.

- Partner with developers and entrepreneurs instead of seeing them as upstarts who don't understand the industry.

- Adopt technology that gathers and analyzes data that is truly helpful to consumers. Don't rely on the last generation of health record systems for data.

- Accept that AI will become an important ally in healthcare and learn to work with it, allowing the technology to do what it does best and professionals to do what they do best.

- Virtualize care. Let cloud-based software help patients when possible and effective, and focus brick-and-mortar facilities on patients who need hands-on care.

- Embrace policy that is good for consumers, because in the long run that will benefit health professionals, even if it means difficult adjustments.

Policymakers

- Relentlessly focus on realigning who decides, who pays and who benefits in healthcare as a pathway to making it more of a consumer-driven free market.

- Create safety-net health assurance so everyone can access good, affordable care. At the same time, develop premium services that might initially be affordable to few but later be available to the masses.

- Understand artificial intelligence. Create regulations governing algorithms, data and privacy before disasters force you to catch up. Consider new ways to regulate AI, like software-defined regulation.

- Recognize the importance of social determinants of health and the fact that 80 percent of a person's healthcare begins at home and involves family, community, food, education and housing. Good healthcare policy involves a lot more than medicine.

- Create the equivalent of a "9-11 commission for healthcare" that starts with the premise that both parties have failed to keep the country healthy at a reasonable cost or safe from this invisible viral enemy.

Insurance Companies

- Invest in changing consumer behavior and become a conduit for health assurance.

- Reimagine the relationship between health assurance and catastrophic health insurance.

- Look for ways to use your data to help customers stay healthier. Focus your business on the consumer instead of on healthcare systems.

- Find new ways to partner with providers and healthcare systems so you share the benefits of cost reductions and better patient experiences created by health assurance.

* * *

This book is a call to action.

Be inspired by the opportunity to think differently about healthcare.

The biggest risk to healthcare is not taking any risks.

That's why a Silicon Valley entrepreneur and a CEO of a 195-year-old academic medical center have something in common.

We both deeply believe it is time for a reinvention of how we deliver care in this country.

And we both know that no one industry can do it alone.

We ask that you as a consumer, provider, insurer, employer, pharmaceutical executive or policymaker look at the events of early 2020 as a call to change how we provide the most important of all human rights: the right to thrive without health problems getting in the way.

ACKNOWLEDGEMENTS

From Hemant Taneja

Thanks to Steve for his leadership and Kevin for his continued collaboration.

To Reva Nohria for her thought partnership. To the entire Commure team, including Brent Dover and Eugene Ketnetsov, for pioneering healthcare innovation. To my partners at GC for their support. To the founders I work closely with as an investor for their creativity and energy.

And to my family—Jess, Bella, Arya, and Ajay.

From Steve Klasko

As an obstetrician, I'm acutely aware that there is a moment of conception and then the birth of a baby nine months later. There are a lot of factors and people in between making sure that the outcome is the best possible. This "baby" began as a chance encounter between Hemant and me over a year ago and there are many people who are responsible for bringing this book to reality.

Phil Green has been my consigliare and initially suggested that Hemant and I might be a good match.

Michael Hoad understands medicine, people and journalism...a great combination if you are writing about a healthcare revolution.

Michael has had a hand in every one of my books and articles and we can almost complete each other's sentences.

John Ekarius has been my chief of staff for over 20 years and has always been there to let me know when I am crossing the line between visionary and crazy...and he's always right.

The board of trustees at Thomas Jefferson University were willing to "think about what will be obvious ten years from now and do it today" as we moved from a hospital company to "healthcare with no address."

Dr. Aimee Van Wynsberghe is leading the global fight to ensure that ethics remain at the forefront of OMO (online meeting offline).

Dayna Bowen Matthew believes that Dr King's admonition, that the greatest form of injustice is healthcare inequities, is still true today and is ready to help the revolution against racial injustice and healthcare disparities.

From Kevin Maney

Thanks, first of all, to Hemant and Steve for being such great partners on this project, and to everyone at General Catalyst and Jefferson who helped in all sorts of ways.

Thanks to my partners at Category Design Advisors, particularly Mike Damphousse, for being patient when this took time away from other work. And to my longtime editing collaborator Bob Roe for giving this a last, sure-handed edit.

Hemant, Steve and Kevin also want to thank all those who helped us understand the healthcare industry and think through health assurance, including: David Goldhill, author of *Catastrophic Care*; Oren Oz, CEO of Nuvo; Andy Thompson, CEO of Proteus Digital Health; Seth Sternberg, CEO of Honor; David Nace, Chief Medical Officer of

Acknowlegdements

Innovaccer; Aneesh Chopra, former Chief Technology Officer of the U.S.; Zach Reitano, CEO of Ro; Othman Laraki, CEO of Color; Marc Harrison, CEO of Intermountain Healthcare; David Nash, founding dean of Jefferson College of Population Health; Glenn Steele, chairman of xG Health Solutions; Rick Bates, CEO of RxSense; and no doubt others we talked to more informally along the way and who were a great help.

INDEX

A

Abundance: The Future is Better Than You Think (Diamandis and Kotler), 2*n*
access to care, 18, 56–57, 70
"Accidents of History Created U.S. Health System" (NPR), 23*n*
administrative costs, 39–40
Aetna, 44, 48
Affordable Care Act (2010), 16, 57, 62
AI. *See* artificial intelligence
Airbnb, 7
airline industry, 68
algorithms, 74–76
Allscripts, 9
always-on physical, 21
Amazon, 3, 40, 49
Ambulnz, 19
American Academy of Family Physicians, 52
American Diabetes Association, 85
analytics platforms, 90
Ancestry, 13–14
annual physical exam, 13
Anthem, 44
Aoun, Adrian, 37
Apple, 3
applied health signals, 27–28

artificial intelligence (AI)
   assisted care and, 92–93
   empathy, not disruption in, 82–83
   growing significance to health, 11–12
   healthcare policy and, 65–66
   policy and technology, 74–76
   traditional medicine and, 41
   wearable gadgets and apps, 14–18
   worker training policy, 73–74
assisted living services, 23
automatic teller machines (ATM), 60
automobile companies, 89–90

B

back-office technology, 90
bandwidth availability, xii
banking regulations, 60
Baylor University Hospital, 24
behavioral health apps, 15–16
Berkshire Hathaway, 49
"Big Bang" solution, 76–77
billing and reimbursement, 64
billing codes, 40, 46, 64
billing software, 56
Blue Button initiative, 66
Blue Cross insurance plan, 24
Blumberg, Alex, 23*n*

Boston Children's Hospital, 80
breakthrough inventions, 68
Brody, Bill, 79
Brohan, Mark, 33n
Buffett, Warren, 49
burnout, workforce, 16, 74
business models
   cash-pay companies, 91
   changing, 7–8, 20–23
   consumer-friendly, 35–36
   fee-for-service, 63–64
   mass production, 4, 7, 22, 25, 28
   out-of-pocket payments, 12, 50–56, 66–67
   third-party, 45–46
   "unscale," 7–8, 25–26, 38, 47

C
Canada, 68
cash-pay companies, 91
Catastrophic Care (Goldhill), 31n, 50
catastrophic health care, 34, 50, 53–55, 96, 103
catastrophic insurance, future of, 96
checks and balances, 46
chronic conditions, 26–27, 36
chronic illness management system, 48
Cigna Insurance, 44–45, 48–49
Clark, Quentin, 79
Cleveland Clinic, 92
clothing retailers, 89–90
Color Genomics, 9, 14, 66
communication skills, 41, 73, 92
communication tools, 61
Commure, 3, 64–65, 67, 78–81
competitive pricing, 46, 56
consumer attitudes, changing, 12, 25, 51–53

consumer-centric health assurance, 34–36, 37–39, 40–41
consumer products companies, 89–90
consumer responsibility, 6–7, 17, 41
consumer segmentation, 21, 38
cost-saving strategies, 49–50
Covid pandemic
   accelerated desire for change, 12
   access to care, 56–57
   data inaccessibility and, 65
   diabetic care and, 27
   economic downturn, 47
   health assurance technologies and, 94–95
   healthcare system problems exposed, 6
   health insurance demographics, 51
   hospital finances and, 63
   insurance coverage loss, 47
   Medicare and telehealth, 72
   New York City hotspot, 88
   rejection of traditional insurance model, 95
   telehealth services, 61
   tipping point, 12
   unemployment filings, 47
   virtualized hospitals and, 72
critical care services, 55–56
Cuomo, Andrew, 88
CVS (Aetna) Insurance, 44–45, 48

D
data
   analytics platforms and, 90
   for artificial intelligence, 75
   automated flow of, 81
   essential nature of, 13
   pandemics and, 99–100
   patient access to, 16–17, 65–66

Index

physiological, 14–15
proprietary algorithms, 76
real-time, 17–18
sharing of, 16
data migration, between apps, 64–65
Davidson, Adam, 23n
decision making, insurance-driven, 50–53
deductibles, 34–35, 37, 44–45, 50–52
deep blood tests, 14
demographics, and changing nature of healthcare, 22
Department of Health and Human Services (HHS), 12
diabetes, 26–27
diabetes spending, 85
Diamandis, Peter, 2n
digital markets, 84–85
digital physicals, 13
direct primary care, 34, 36–38, 51–52
direct-purchase insurance, 44
disruption *vs.* partnership, 83–84
DNA, 13–14
doctor appointments, changing nature of, 19
doctor–patient relationship, 13, 17–19, 22, 82, 87
drugs, 20

E

economies of scale, 22–23, 26–27, 48–49
efficiency *vs.* efficacy, 85–86
electronic medical records (EMR), 16, 40, 79, 82, 87
empathy, AI and, 82–83
empathy at scale, 21, 23–24
employee retention, 54–55
employer health benefits, 24–25, 50, 54–55
entrepreneurial opportunities
cost *vs.* user experience, 50–52
Covid-inspired, 11–12, 89–93
health policy and, 60–62, 68–69
successful startups, 47–50
tech–healthcare challenges, 5–6
transparency and competition, 56
erectile dysfunction, 35, 58–59
Express Scripts, 23, 48–49

F

family physicians, 22, 36, 41, 83
Fast Healthcare Interoperability Resources (FHIR), 11–12, 17, 80
Federation of State Medical Boards, 59
fee-for-service model, 63–64, 84, 88
FHIR standard, 11–12, 17, 80
flat fee *vs.* traditional insurance, 37–38, 52, 55, 102
Forward, 36–38, 87–88
free-market economics, 2, 50–53, 80, 102

G

Gallup National Health and Well-Being Index, 51
General Catalyst, 39, 79
genetic testing, 13–14, 36
genomics, 13–15, 66, 97. *See also* Color Genomics
Goldhill, David, 31n, 50, 51, 57
Google, 3
Grail, 14
Grove, Andy, 11

H

Harrison, Marc, 34
Haven, 49, 83–84
health, as a financial asset, 53–55

health, wholistic nature of, 96
Health Affairs study, 40
health assurance
    access to care, 56–57
    AI policy and, 73–74, 74–75, 75–76
    benefits of transformation, 41–42, 52
    business opportunity, 29–30
    capitalization of, 17–18
    chronic conditions and, 52
    concept of, 1–2, 40
    consumer-first, 67
    consumer responsibility and control, 97
    data and, 65–66
    economics of healthcare, 48
    employee retention and, 54–55
    employer health benefits and, 54–55
    financial implications of, 53–57
    future of, 97
    innovative thinking for, 69
    insurance-driven decision making, 50–53
    investor funding of, 35
    as new experience, 12–13
    pricing transparency and, 20–21, 56
    principles of policy design, 62–76
    promises of, 4–5
    sectors threatened by transformation, 42
    vs. status quo, 71–72
    workforce retention and training, 73–74
health assurance accounts, 95–96
health assurance companies, 78–81, 82–89. *See also individual company names*
healthcare
    administrative costs of, 39–40
    affordability of, 32
    communication, 92
    as a craft, 22
    demographics and changing nature of, 22
    insurance and billing complexities, 12, 46
    providers, 4
    segmentation of, 85
    technology innovation, 3, 23
healthcare allowance option, 54–55
healthcare apps
    behavioral, 15–16
    Commure and, 64–65
    early startups, 5–6
    future use of, 96
    Mindstrong, 63–64
    policy development and, 63–64, 70–71
    shared data and, 11–12, 14–15, 90
healthcare industry
    empathy and, 82–83
    legacy, 71–73
    technological reinvention of, 12–13
    traditional approach, 63
    workforce retention and retraining, 73–74
healthcare innovation
    affordability of, 68–69
    blended skills needed for, 78–80
    diabetes and, 26, 85
    electronic health records and, 87
    leadership teams and, 62
    vs. Medicare for all, 57
    to minimize healthcare, 87
    policy and, 64–65
    regulation and, 70–71
    tech approach to, 85, 101
    tech investment for, 3
healthcare policy design
    access to affordable care, 68–69

Index

artificial intelligence and, 74–76
"Big Bang" solution, 76–77
consumer responsibility for data, 65–66
design principles debate, 62
digital technology and, 61–62
disruption and innovation in, 62
open innovation, 64–65
patients as informed consumers, 66–67
retraining of professionals and workers, 73–74
reward for health, not sickness, 63–64
Ro case study, 58–59
safety *vs.* efficacy, 70–71
state licensing requirements, 59–61
status quo *vs.* health assurance, 71–73
healthcare resiliency, 88–89
healthcare systems, 2, 4, 11, 31
healthcare–tech partnership, 83–84
"healthcare with no address" strategy, 8, 9, 39, 72, 80
"health hub" strategy, 48–49
health insurance
    changing demographics of, 51
    changing nature of, 20–21
    consumer abandonment of, 91
    cost escalation, 50–51
    Covid pandemic changes in, 72
    Covid pandemic consumer losses, 47
    for critical care, 55–56
    digital markets and, 42
    economies of scale and, 49
    employer–employee cost sharing, 50
    health assurance transformation and, 42
    high-deductible plans, 51–52
    Kaiser Permanents plan, 33
    limitations and cost of traditional, 12
    medical specialties and, 41
    negotiated prices and, 31, 46
    new role for, 72, 103
    origins of, 23–25
    Oscar's role in, 55
    outcomes and payment, 30–31
    policy changes for, 87–88
    popular scorn for, 42–43
    pricing transparency and, 66–67
    rejection of traditional, 95
    Ro and Livongo challenges to, 48
    as third-party payers, 30
    user experience and, 23–24
health insurance industry, traditional, 43–46
health outcomes, payment for, 30–31
health policy, politicians and, 31
health provider behavior, 46
high-deductible plans, 51–54, 95–96
hospice services, 23
hospital finances, regulations protecting, 31
hospital mergers, 22–23
hospital subsidies, 72
hospital systems, transformation of, 42
household income, insurance coverage and, 51–52
Humana Insurance, 44–45

I

ingestible chips, 20
insomnia, 35
insurance and billing complexities, 12, 46
insurance-driven decision making, 50–53
Intermountain Healthcare, 34

J

JeffConnect, 34–35, 39
Jefferson Health

health assurance and, 17–18
Livongo and, 26–27
merger opportunities, 23, 49
origin and transformation of, 8
service for obstetric patients, 67
viability strategy, 38–39
joint ventures, 83
JPMorgan Chase, 49

K
Kaiser Permanente, 33–34
Keckley, Paul, 32
Khan Academy, 7
Kinsa thermometers, x
Klasko, Steve
 a-ha! moment, 27
 Commure and, 78–81
 Covid crisis and, 39, xi–xii
 General Catalyst and, 39
 Jefferson Health and, 8–9, 17–18, 23, 38–39
 Livongo and, 9, 27–28
 partnership with Hemant Taneja, 7
Klasko's Conundrum, 8–9
knee replacement, 21, 54
Kotler, Steven, 2n
Kuznetsov, Eugene, 79–80

L
Labcorp, 23
legacy healthcare industry, 71–73
legislation
 21st Century Cures Act, (2016), 65
 Affordable Care Act (2010), 16, 57, 62
 Riegle-Neal Interstate Banking and Branching Efficiency Act (1994), 60
licensing, state medical, 59–62
lifespan, average U.S., 4

Livongo Health, Inc.
 artificial intelligence and, 66, 82–83
 chronic conditions and, 15, 36
 diabetes and, 26
 example of new business model, 3
 founders, 9, 26
 outside insurance-driven norm, 48
 safety–efficacy tension, 70–71

M
Maney, Kevin *Unscaled*, 22n
market leadership, 84–85
market-segment personas, 86
mass production business model, 4, 7, 22, 25, 28
Mayo Clinic, 44
Medicaid, 44, 66
medical licensing, 59–62
medical loss ratio, 30
medical specialties, 41
Medicare, 44, 72
Medicare for all, 57, 61–62, 69
medications, 20
memorized knowledge, 41
mental health, 15–16
mergers and acquisitions, 48–49
Merlo, Larry, 48
microbiome, 14, 17
Microsoft, 3
military insurance, 44
Mindstrong Health, 9, 15, 63–64
movie industry revolution, 72–73

N
Narayana Health, 54
National Academy of Medicine, 74
national health care system, 24

negotiated prices, 31, 46
Netflix, 25
New York City, 88
Nuvo, Inc., 53–54, 94

O
ongoing medical conditions, 55
Only the Paranoid Survive (Grove), 11n
open data, 65
open-source software, 76
Oscar, 55
out-of-pocket payments, 12, 50–51, 53–54, 56, 66–67

P
pandemics, health assurance and, 97–100. *See also* Covid pandemic
partnership *vs.* disruption, 83–84
patients, as consumers, 53, 66–67
payers, health system, 30
payment incentives, alignment of, 87–88
payment processing, 90
pediatricians, 41, 86
perpetual digital physical, 13
pharmaceutical companies, 42, 72
pharmacy licensing, 60
Philadelphia, telehealth in, xii
physical exams, 13–14, 17–20, 19–20
physician burnout, 16
physician practices, hospital ownership of, 23
physiological data, 14–15
pregnancy and childbirth, 53–54, 67
premium services, 20, 38, 54, 68–69, 102
pre-primary care, 17–18
price competition, 50–51, 54, 60, 66–67
price sensitivity, income and, 51–52

pricing transparency
  checks and balances, 46
  deciding, paying, benefiting, 45–48, 50–52, 57, 87–88, 95, 102
  health assurance and, 20–21
  health assurance examples, 34–36
  income level price sensitivity and, 51
  informed decision making and, 30–31, 56, 66–67
  pharmaceutical company, 42
  sector *vs.* sector combat, 32
primary care services
  budgeting for, 54–55
  vs. critical care, 55–56
  direct, 51–52
  Forward, 36–38
  Intermountain Healthcare and, 34
  JeffConnect and, 34–35
  market segmentation and, 86
  ongoing medical conditions and, 55
  segmentation for, 86
  subscription model for, 17, 34, 87
  virtual, 36
privacy, patient, 59, 92, 98, 99
privacy laws, data access and, 66, 103
private healthcare, in Canada, 68
procedure codes, 40
proprietary algorithms and data, 76
Proteus Digital Health, 20
PTSD, healthcare workers and, 15–16

Q
Quest Diagnostics, 23

R
Rahmanian, Saman, 59
real-time data, 17–18
Reed, Mary, 33–34

regulation, software-defined, 75
regulatory approval, 70
Reitano, Zach, 58–59
remote care, pandemics and, 98–99
resiliency, healthcare, 88–89
resource sharing, 34, 88, 99
retail, virtualized, 40
retention and training, 73–74
Roman, 59
Ro telehealth
   an unscaled company, 47
   consumer-friendly business model, 35–36
   enrollment process, 47
   example of new technology, 3
   origin of, 58–59
routine care
   vs. direct primary care, 51–52
   future of, 95–96
   genetic testing and, 14
   health assurance accounts and, 95–96
   insurance for, 51–52
   Nuvo and, 53–54

S

safety–efficacy tension, 70
Sanders, Bernie, 57
scaling up, 30
scaling up paradox, 80
Schlosser, Mario, 55
Schutz, Rob, 59
scribes, for EMR, 87
self-insurance management, 91
Sesame, Inc., 51, 86, 91
sick care
   alternative to, 3, 12–13
   vs. health assurance, 78, 84, 85
   policy changes needed, 63–64
   recasting of, 29–30
   transition to health assurance, 40–41
Silicon Valley startups, 5–6, 39–40, 78–79, 83–84
Singh, Inder, x
skeleton keys, health data and, 17
skilled nursing facilities, 23
smartphone innovation, 71
societal health, 56–57
software. *See also* healthcare apps
   AI-driven bots, 74
   artificial intelligence and, 18, 36–37
   billing, 56
   interoperability of, 65
   Livongo, 27, 70
   open-source, 76
   skeleton key, 17
   wearable, 96, 98–99
software-defined regulation, 75–76
Spire, 15
static data, 14, 17–18
strategic inflection point, 11
stress, healthcare workers and, 15–16
Stripe payments platform, 79, 90
subscription service, healthcare as, 20, 23–24, 34, 36–38, 87–88
success, measurement by disengagement, 87
supply and demand, 46

T

Taneja, Hemant
   Covid pandemic and, xii
   early investor in Stripe, 90
   founding of Commure, 8, 78–81
   founding of Livongo, 26
   partnership with Steve Klasko, 7
   Unscaled, 22n

Index

targeted markets, 89–90
tech–healthcare partnership, 83–84
tech industry, empathy and, 82–83
telecommunications industry, 69
telehealth services, 6, 31, 34, 61, 72, ix–xii
telehealth successes, 34–35
third-party payer business model, 45–46
traditional healthcare
    mergers and acquisitions, 48–49
    obsolescence of, 94
traditional insurance, origins of, 24
traditional insurance vs. healthcare allowance, 54–55
training and retention, 73–74
Trump administration, 61
Tullman, Glen, 9, 26
21st Century Cures Act, (2016), 65
23andMe, 14, 66

U
Uber, 25
UnitedHealth, 44, 45
"unscale" business model, 7–8, 25–26, 38, 47
Unscaled (Taneja and Maney), 22*n*
unscheduled care costs, 34–35
user experience
    for chronic conditions, 26–27
    economies of scale and, 23–24
    income levels and, 51–52
    Livongo and, 36, 48
    origins of, 21–22, 25
    rise of insurance, 23–24
    Ro and, 35–36, 47
user satisfaction, 43, 46

V
van Lamoen, Diede, 79
Veterans Administration, 66
virtual care, Livongo and, 27
virtual medical practice, 36–38, 41, 59–62, 72, 80, ix

W
Wachter, Bob, 79
wage growth *vs.* health insurance spending, 50
waiting rooms, 19, 27
Warby Parker, 3
watchdog algorithms, 75–76
Watson (IBM), 92
who decides, pays, benefits, 45–48, 51–55, 57, 87–88, 95, 102
winner-take-all mentality, 84–85
workforce realignment, 92
workforce retention and training, 73–74

Z
ZocDoc, 19

Hemant Taneja is the executive chairman and co-founder of Commure. He is also a managing director at the venture capital firm General Catalyst and has been featured on the Forbes Midas List of top venture investors. He partners with mission-driven founders building platform companies that are fundamentally aligned with the long-term interests of society. He and General Catalyst are early investors in companies including Airbnb, Color, Grammarly, Gusto, Livongo, Mindstrong, Oscar, Ro Health, Samsara, Snap, Stripe, and Warby Parker. In 2018, Hemant published *Unscaled*, his first book, which outlines his investment thesis of "economies of unscale."

Dr. Stephen Klasko is president of Thomas Jefferson University and CEO of Jefferson Health. In 2020, the World Economic Forum named him a Distinguished Fellow for the Digital Economy and New Value Creation. For three years he has been listed among the most influential people by *Modern Healthcare* and was the only healthcare executive listed in *Fast Company*'s "most creative people in business."

Kevin Maney is a best-selling author, technology journalist, and a founding partner of Category Design Advisors. His previous books include *Unscaled*, co-authored with Hemant, and *Play Bigger: How Pirates, Dreamers and Innovators Create and Dominate Markets* and *The Maverick and His Machine: Thomas Watson Sr. and the Making of IBM*. He has written for dozens of media outlets, including *USA Today*, *Fortune*, *Wired* and *Newsweek*, and appeared regularly on television and radio, including CNN, CNBC, NPR and CBS Sunday Morning.

PRAISE FOR UNHEALTHCARE

"Can we create a health system that rewards health instead of sickness, embraces innovation, and puts consumers in charge? This book gives a crisp prescription on how, by shifting from a system based on scarcity to one based on abundance. And with COVID-19 as healthcare's 'iPhone moment,' now is the time to act."
— PETER LEE Corporate Vice President, Microsoft Research

"Taneja and Klasko's brilliance is in the power of rethinking what's possible and no doubt required for the future of healthcare."
— DAVID SHULKIN, MD Former Secretary, U.S. Department of Veterans Affairs

"Steve and Hemant brilliantly explain that while the healthcare dilemma seems insurmountable, it really isn't."
— JOHN SCULLEY Former Apple CEO

"UnHealthcare offers us a hopeful path that consumers, aided with smarter decision support, will access a delivery system that competes on keeping us healthy."
— ANEESH CHOPRA Former U.S. Chief Technology Officer

"Steve and Hemant have come together to challenge us to rethink what's possible for healthcare if we are willing to move beyond our traditional approach."
— VALERIE MONTGOMERY RICE, MD President and Dean, Morehouse School of Medicine

"This book offers an insightful blueprint for what needs to change and how best to harness the transformative forces in technology and AI to have healthcare join the consumer revolution."
— MOIRA FORBES Publisher, *ForbesWoman*

CPSIA information can be obtained
at www.ICGtesting.com
Printed in the USA
BVHW032224280421
606021BV00001BB/33

9 781716 996511